DRY BASEMENT SCIENCE

What to Have Done and Why

Lawrence Janesky

Dry Basement Science
What to Have Done and Why

by Lawrence Janesky

Published by:
Basement Systems, Inc.
60 Silvermine Road, Seymour, CT 06483
800-640-1500
203-881-5090

ISBN: 0-9776457-1-1

2nd Edition.

edited by Richard Fencil

Visit us at www.basementsystems.com

This book is dedicated to the hard-working men and women at Basement Systems dealerships worldwide, who solve the mystery of how to make comfortable, dry, usable space out of wet or damp basements for homeowners everyday.

Table of Contents

Forward

This is not a do-it-yourself book because basement waterproofing is not a do-it-yourself job. It's hard work, and takes too much specialized knowledge, skill, and equipment.

The purpose of this book is to give you enough knowledge to make an educated decision on how to know what work needs to be done to your home, who to do it, and why.

Dry Basement Science. Don't let the title fool you. It's not that complicated. In fact, you will see why I nearly called the book "Dry Basements – When Science Meets Common Sense".

What qualifies me to write this book? I am the founder and president of Basement Systems Inc, the world's largest basement waterproofing company. Since the beginning, Basement Systems has actively sought better ways of doing things. We are not the kind of company that has a single year of experience 20 times; rather we are a learning organization, hell bent on seeking the best way.

Basement Systems has developed a close network of like-minded basement waterproofing contractors that are dealers of our products (one of them probably gave you this book). We have more than 240 dealers in seven countries, some with more experience than me, who install the best basement waterproofing products and systems ever developed. We are not saying these products are the best because they are ours – but rather they are ours because they are the best. Without our more-than-significant efforts toward creating better ways of fixing wet basements, most of these products would not exist, as we are the inventors and developers of them.

Because we work with so many basement waterproofing experts every day, and fix thousands of wet basements ourselves (we fixed 2,474 wet basements from our Connecticut office alone in 2004), we bring you the collective wisdom of thousands of experts and hundreds of thousands of jobs completed. It's all we do and we love it. That's what makes me an expert.

Basement waterproofing as a business has been around since the 1930's or 40's. Not a lot of new thinking has been applied until 1990 or so. Almost every other home improvement sector or appliance that you use has been modernized, changed and improved. Now it's time for basement waterproofing to come of age.

CAUTION

Watch out for old ideas still offered that don't work all the time.

Your basement is useful space, easy to heat and cool, and easy to finish. And a home buyer will expect your basement to be dry. Since you can spend a lot of money and not get the result you wanted, this is an important subject.

And if it's worth owning a home with a wet basement at all, it is certainly worth fixing...

Basement Environment Specialists®

What Do You Want?

Take the Quiz –

Important

Finish the next two thoughts by choosing A, B, or C.

I want –

❏ A) Part of my basement dry
   You probably already have this, you can stop reading now.

❏ B) Most of my basement dry
   Then only treat part of your basement.

☑ C) My WHOLE basement dry!
   Then treat your WHOLE basement.

I want a dry basement –

❏ A) When it doesn't rain.
   You probably already have this, you can stop reading now.

❏ B) Most of the time.
   You probably have a dry basement most of the time like most wet basement sufferers. You can make it worse by spending SOME money on it, fix it halfway, and you will still have a dry basement only most of the time. (Arghhhh!)

☑ C) ALL the time!
   Then have it fixed right. Don't cheap out.

So the premise of this book is that you want your <u>whole</u> basement dry <u>all</u> the time. Read on…

How to Use this Book
A Reader's Guide

There are 14 brief chapters, each dealing with a specific aspect of achieving your dry basement goal (See the Table of Contents). There are photographs and sidebars in each chapter to help communicate a point. In addition there are eight different symbols which have different meanings-

This is especially important for finished basements.

The two products or systems discussed are very different.

This is important!

Additional Information

This subject is very important in getting the results you want.

You will love the results from this!

Beware, don't make this mistake.

This is industry insider information.

Basement Terms of the Trade

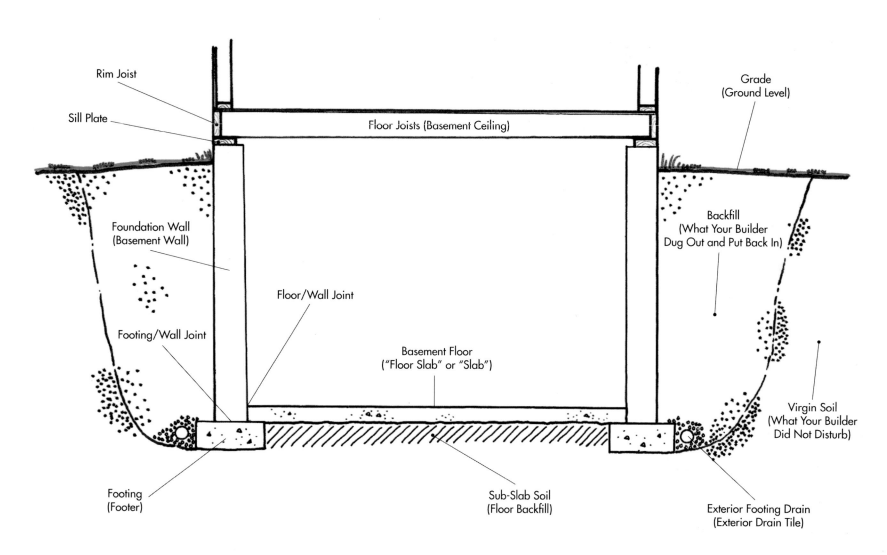

Rim Joist

Sill Plate

Grade (Ground Level)

Floor Joists (Basement Ceiling)

Foundation Wall (Basement Wall)

Backfill (What Your Builder Dug Out and Put Back In)

Floor/Wall Joint

Footing/Wall Joint

Basement Floor ("Floor Slab" or "Slab")

Footing (Footer)

Virgin Soil (What Your Builder Did Not Disturb)

Sub-Slab Soil (Floor Backfill)

Exterior Footing Drain (Exterior Drain Tile)

Chapter 1

Your Basement is Valuable Space!

Mr. and Mrs. Wetmore had a home with a wet basement. For many years they chose to add optimism to the problem, saying it would go away due to various factors that the gods would put in their favor. Several times each year the air was filled with the sound of their wet vac, and grumbles of another "freak" situation. Some years later when trying to sell their home, the Wetmore's found that once a potential buyer liked their home and got to the basement or inspection stage, they walked away, not wanting to inherit someone else's problem they viewed as unsolvable. Hence, the Wetmore's couldn't sell their home.

Mr. and Mrs. Rainwater's basement flooded once. They cleaned the gutters just like their cousin told them to. After all, he was a builder and he knew about these things. They didn't see any more water in their basement for a good six months. They soon forgot about the incident and put all their stuff on the basement floor. There was holiday stuff, tax records, a record album collection, personal effects – even Mrs. Rainwater's preserved wedding dress – in a cardboard box like most of the other items. Beginning one otherwise peaceful evening, the sky opened up, as it does once every year or two, and two months of rain fell in two days. All the Rainwater's belongings were lost in the flood that resulted in the unprotected basement.

Mr. Gill wanted some space to call his own. The kids were getting older and taking up lots of space and making lots of noise upstairs. So he hired **Billy Doright**, carpenter extraordinaire, to finish the basement. "Does the basement ever leak," Billy asked? "Not really," said Mr. Gill. So Billy hammered and dry walled, and painted for weeks, finishing just in time for the Carpet World guys installation date. Mr. Gill was so proud. One crisp morning Mr. Gill decided to run down to the basement to gaze at his new sanctuary for inspiration before going to work. He never made it to work. Instead he spent the day on the phone with his insurance company, only to find that his newly finished, and even more newly ruined finished basement was not covered by insurance. "Groundwater leaks are never covered" – the words echoed in his head for weeks.

Mr. and Mrs. Spore moved their three small children into a new-to-them home. They knew the basement "had some issues," but felt they could deal with that later. After some time, two of the children began having asthma-like symptoms. When they went to school, they were better. When they came home they puffed up again, and stuff leaked from their faces. What was in the home that was causing it? After hiring a Indoor Air Quality consultant, they found the cause – mold in the basement from the slight but chronic seepage. "We can get rid of the mold," the expert said. "Will it grow back?" asked Mrs. Spore. If the basement still leaks it could grow back the expert said. And so it did. Mrs. Spore dealt with the mold issue by having her pediatrician prescribe these great allergy drugs to feed to her children to keep the symptoms at bay.

Mrs. Soker lived with her basement water problem for all of her forty years in the home at 14 Elm Street. She just couldn't see spending more than a few hundred dollars to fix it, and all the "experts" wanted much more than that. "Don't do it Ma" her concerned son advised by phone from Seattle. "They're just trying to take advantage of you, being a widow and all." So she lived with it. Years later, when her surviving son Mr. Soker flew in to handle the executors duties, he was told by the real estate agent that the only way that the home could be sold was to fix the basement properly. So he did, using the funds from the estate. Poor Mrs. Soker. For 52 years she had to put up with a wet basement.

Mrs. Soker's neighbor, **Mrs. Wright**, took a different road. She had her basement properly fixed long ago, and she was spared the financial and emotional cost that became the fate of her dear neighbor. "If I knew about this before, I'd have fixed it 15 years ago" was her only regret.

Prove it!

Do this test. In the winter, go into your basement and open a window a bit. Feel the cold air blasting in at you? Close the window.

Now go upstairs – to the second floor if you have one. Crack open a window an inch or so. You don't feel any cold air blasting in? Why not? Because warm air is blasting OUT.

With low air pressure on the lower levels, your house sucks on the ground, then blows air out of the upper levels due to a higher air pressure.

You Breathe Basement Air
Like it or Not

As warm air rises in a home it leaks out of the upper levels. New air must enter to replace the air that escaped. In fact, in a tight home about half of the air in the home escapes each hour out of the upper levels. This creates a suction at the lower levels of the home to draw in replacement air. In older leaky homes the air exchange rate can be as high as two air exchanges per hour.

What this "stack effect" does is create an airflow in your home from bottom to top. So air from the basement is drawn upwards into the first floor, and then to the second floor. Of course it dilutes with other air in your home, but building scientists say that up to 50% of the air you breathe on the first floor is air that came from the basement. If you have hot air heating with ductwork, the air mixes even more thoroughly throughout the house.

Therefore, whatever is in your basement air is in your house and affecting you, whether you spend much time in the basement or not. If there is high humidity downstairs, there is higher humidity upstairs than there would be otherwise. If there is mold in the basement, there are mold spores upstairs. If there are damp odors downstairs – you get the idea.

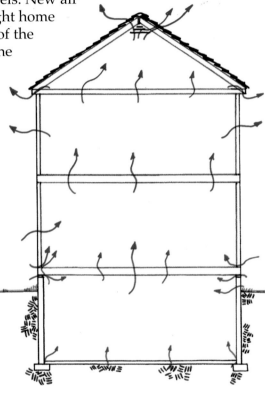

STACK EFFECT

To Your Health
(And if not yours, then theirs)

You can't find a doctor who says mold in a home is good. You can't find a doctor who says mold in your home is "not bad." It's bad. It's all bad.

Besides irritating people with asthma and mold allergies, studies show that prolonged exposure to mold can actually cause asthma.

Mold = Bad

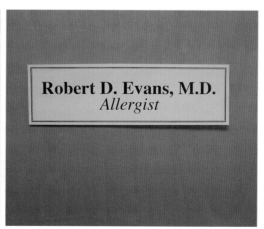

Robert D. Evans, M.D.
Allergist

Dust Mites
#1 Indoor Allergen

Dust Mites are parasites that live in your carpeting, bedding and furniture. They are tiny – you can't see them. Their droppings are even smaller, and float in the air. These droppings are the number one thing people with asthma and allergies react to indoors.

What you need to know about dust mites is that they don't drink water, but instead absorb water out of the air. When the relative humidity is more than 50%, dust mites thrive. When the relative humidity goes down below 50%, they dry up and die (however, they leave their larvae behind to hatch when it gets damp again.). Of course when they die, they stop pooping. So the best way to combat dust mites is to dry up your wet basement and then keep the relative humidity down below 50%.

See chapter 8 for more on humidity control.

"Just Add Water"
Negative Effects of a Wet or Damp Basement

Since air flows upward into the upper levels of your home from the basement, it brings the humidity from the basement with it. The effects on your home can include:

◆ Dust Mites (the number one indoor allergen)
◆ Sticking (swollen) doors and windows
◆ Smelly damp carpets
◆ Buckling hardwood floors
◆ Condensation/rotting/mold in your attic (as humid air escapes into your attic it can condense against the cold ceiling or roof)
◆ Frost or condensation and mold on the inside of windows in cool weather
◆ Increased cooling bills (damp air takes more energy to cool)
◆ Increased heating bills (damp air takes more energy to heat)
◆ Mold upstairs
◆ Decreased life of roof sheathing and shingles
◆ Decreased life of the paint on the outside of your house
◆ Aggravated asthma and allergies

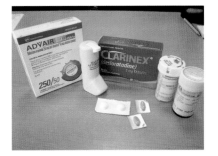

The damage in the basement itself is obvious. The above list represents many of the effects that can happen upstairs that you may not associate with your wet or damp basement.

Your Basement
Extra Space for Living!

What can you do with your basement?

Playroom • Billiard Room • Party Room • Family Room/Den/TV Room • Art Room • Teen Bedroom • Home Office • Bedrooms • In-Law Apartment • Home Gym • Potting Room • Model Train Set • Home Theater • Library • Wine Cellar • Extra Bathroom • Sauna • Record Storage • Sewing Room • Basement Bar • Computer Room • Cedar Closet • Arts/Crafts Room

Buyers Expect a Dry Basement

Who wants to buy a home with a wet basement? Nobody! It's difficult enough to find a buyer who wants your house, and heart-breaking when they walk away after looking at the basement.

These days in most states there are disclosure forms which ask the seller a whole range of questions about their knowledge of defects with the property. One of the questions asks if you ever had any water in the basement. In addition, most buyers hire home inspectors these days to inspect the property for defects. Home inspectors have a keen eye for water problems because that's what they are hired for.

There is simply no hiding your wet basement when you sell your home. And if you do disclose your leaky basement, either nobody will buy, or they will make a low offer. In fact, buyers will discount the price of a home by 10% or more because of a wet basement.

10% is a lot of money!

Because buyers view your home with a wet basement as a fixer-upper, they will pay you 10% less than otherwise – that's if they buy it at all. Using this example then –

If your home is worth-	The cost of not fixing your wet basement in property value alone is-
$100,000	$10,000
$150,000	$15,000
$200,000	$20,000
$300,000	$30,000
$400,000	$40,000
$500,000	$50,000
$600,000	$60,000

You get the idea. And this does not take into account all the property damage and other aggravation that the leak causes you while you live there!

Moral of the Story
–Fixing your wet basement is a lot cheaper than not fixing your wet basement!

Basement Space is Cheaper Than Addition Space

To get more space in your home you can put an addition on at around $50 to $100 a square foot, or finish the basement at $10 to $20 per square foot. Now there's a bargain! But you can't finish your basement if it's wet – not even a little bit wet, not even a little bit of the time!

Even Unfinished Space = Finished

So you're not going to finish your basement you say? Well, your unfinished space is just as valuable as finished space – why? Because all your stuff that you'd normally put in your dry unfinished basement is now upstairs taking up finished space! It's crammed in the closets, the spare room, and the garage. By drying the basement you can move all that stuff downstairs and reclaim your finished space!

Spend More/Costs Less

Do the Math

Pick Your Situation Below

Expensive Area
One Story Home

Your home
$350,000 - 2400 square feet
Wet basement, only 1200 sq.ft. usable

Add $8,000 to fix basement

Total cost $358,000
2400 square feet usable

The Math
$350,000/1200=**$291** per usable sq. ft.

$358,000/2400=**$149** per usable sq. ft.

Expensive Area
Two Story Home

Your home
$450,000 - 3000 square feet
Wet basement, only 2000 sq.ft. usable

Add $8,000 to fix basement

Total cost $458,000
3000 square feet usable

The Math
$450,000/2000=**$225** per usable sq. ft.

$458,000/3000=**$152** per usable sq. ft.

Less Expensive Area
One Story Home

Your home
$120,000 - 2400 square feet
Wet basement, only 1200 sq.ft. usable

Add $8,000 to fix basement

Total cost $128,000
2400 square feet usable

The Math
$120,000/1200=**$100** per usable sq. ft.

$128,000/2400=**$53** per usable sq. ft.

Less Expensive Area
Two Story Home

Your home
$210,000 - 3000 square feet
Wet basement, only 2000 sq.ft. usable

Add $8,000 to fix basement

Total cost $218,000
3000 square feet usable

The Math
$350,000/1200=**$105** per usable sq. ft.

$218,000/3000=**$73** per usable sq. ft.

Chapter 2

Why Basements Leak

Designed for Failure

When builders build homes, they have a lot of things to put in the house and pay for. Given the choice of spending money on beautiful things like great cabinets and bathroom fixtures, or on things that protect the house and make it last longer that a buyer won't see – he goes for the beauty. Why? It's what people see and want.

There are two things that keep a basement from leaking.

    1) A coating on the basement walls

    2) A proper drain around the bottom of the foundation – called a "footing drain"

Wall coatings can be inexpensive black tar coatings called "dampproofing". Dampproofing costs builders about 20 cents per square foot or around $200 a home. Dampproofing doesn't bridge wall cracks, doesn't stop water completely, and doesn't last forever. Until about 1985, nearly all new homes were dampproofed.

Bling Bling.
Buyers want things that are visible and look nice.

Foundation dampproofing.

14

Waterproof coating.

Even today, 85% of homes still only get their foundation walls dampproofed.

A big step up from dampproofing is "Waterproof" coatings. These will cost a builder from 60 cents per square foot to $1.25 per square foot or $1000 or more per home. It often includes some kind of drainage board or protection board, such as foam, over them. Waterproofing will bridge most small wall cracks, and will last a lot longer than dampproofing.

Footing drains are plastic pipes with holes or slots laid around the outside of the footing or at the bottom of the walls. A bed of crushed stone is installed around them and the soil around the outside of your home is pushed back over the drains. There are many things that can go wrong with a footing drain – especially since unskilled labor is often used to install them.

Problems include –

♦ The drains don't lead out anywhere – fairly common
♦ The place they lead off to is blocked, clogged or crushed— fairly common
♦ The drains clog as the water washing into them brings silt and sediment (mud) with it – extremely common
♦ The drains have very little or no stone around them – stone is expensive.
♦ The drains are not connected as a continuous loop or are installed too high.
♦ Etc. etc.

Footing Drain Failure

Footing drain failure is the most common cause of wet basements. When this happens – the soil around the outside of the foundation can't drain and it becomes saturated. The weight of the water in the soil creates hydrostatic pressure, and pushes the water into the basement through:

❖The joint between the footing and the wall – most common

❖Through wall cracks and pipe penetrations – very common

❖Through porous block walls – very common if you have block walls.

❖Under the footing – pretty rare

Big "IFs." *Exterior footing drains work* **if** *installed properly and* **if** *they don't clog.*

Stone under the floor is helpful.

2

By installing stone aggregate under the floor instead of just dirt, the builder can help water that does get under the floor drain to a sump location. There are

also inexpensive drainage flashings such as "CactusBoard" Floor Edging that builders can install around the perimeter of the floor. The problem is that stone can cost $400 - $600 per home and $100 for drainage flashing at the floor/ wall joint. And usually, no bling bling – no go.

Foundation Types

Poured Concrete Walls

❖ Most common today.

Concrete Block Walls

❖ Most common 1940-1975. Still used today.

Foundation Types

Stone Walls
❖ Common in older homes.

Monolithic Foundations
❖ Could be block or poured walls.
❖ The difference is that the floor and footing are poured in one piece.
❖ With the walls on top, it's a two-piece foundation instead of a three piece.

Precast Foundation Walls
❖ Newest idea, still relatively rare.

Wood Foundation Walls
❖ Treated wood stud walls and plywood.
❖ Very rare in most areas.

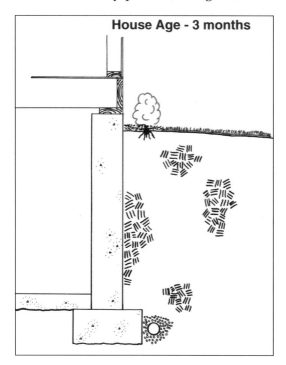

Janesky's First Law of Hydrodynamics –

Water flows downhill.

Dirt Around a Foundation Settles

When the loose soil is pushed back against a new foundation, it will settle – especially in the first few years. This doesn't help a wet basement situation, and dirt should be added so water does not flow towards the foundation. Unlike dirt, mulch is porous and water easily passes through it, so mulch doesn't count.

Anything But Average

It's no secret that wet weather floods basements. But dry weather is a part of the problem too. In periods of drought, the soil shrinks away from the foundation, leaving

voids for the next rain to easily flow down into your basement before they close up. Average rainfall means an average of wet periods and dry periods.

Hydrostatic Pressure

Hydrostatic Pressure is pressure from a body of water at rest. The weight of the water itself is what causes the pressure. The higher the water is in a vertical column, the more the pressure. So if the void space in the soil outside of your foundation is filled with water (temporarily during a rain) it will cause hydrostatic pressure to push the water into your basement. The higher the soil is filled, the more the pressure.

It's simple.

Your basement is a hole in the ground lined with an imperfect concrete structure – a porous material with cracks, holes, and joints in it. That's why basements leak.

Imperfect Fit. *First, footings are poured and after these set, walls are poured on top, leaving a joint through which water can enter.*

Chapter 3

Outer Limits
What Can (or should) Be Done Outside

(If you aren't thinking about digging it up outside, you can skip this section)

One way to fix a wet basement is to dig up the earth outside around your foundation and waterproof the walls and install a new footing drain. This is almost never a good option. Why?

First of all you'll be replacing the same system that failed you – and how long will it last this time?

The big problem is the excavation itself. You have to dig down to the bottom of the footing, about 8 feet deep. Picture standing in a trench, looking up at where the grass used to be. An 8-foot deep trench has to be at least 8 feet wide at the top (12 feet if you ask OSHA).

And where will all that dirt that comes out of the hole go? It's piled up in the rest of your yard. You can expect about 25 feet of your yard all the way around your home to be destroyed.

Everything in this area has to be removed and replaced, including porches, driveways, sidewalks, landscaping, air conditioning units, decks, steps, and so on. Then after the work is done, the dirt that was excavated – which is now fluffed up and loose on your lawn, is put back in the trench. It will take years for this dirt to settle, and as it does, new dirt has to be added against the foundation to keep the slope away from the house. Then you can put your driveway, sidewalks, decks, porches, and landscaping back. This is reason enough not to consider doing the job outside.

If you need more reason to dismiss this dastardly idea, how about these:

1. Where will the drain go to? If you don't have a lot of slope on your property to take the pipe out to daylight, then you need to bring the pipe inside the foundation to a sump pump anyway.

2. Exterior Excavation does not address water vapor coming through your basement walls and floor.

3. Nor does this method address humidity – and won't ensure that mold won't grow either.

4. What if something goes wrong and there is still a little seepage? What will you do then? Dig it all up again? Outside systems are not serviceable.

5. It costs a lot of money – like up to $20,000 to go all the way around your home!

I think we can close the book on this option.

Grading

If the soil around your foundation is pitched towards the foundation, it's a good idea to add dirt so that the soil slopes away. Be sure not to use sand or mulch, because water flows right down through these materials whether they are pitched or not. It's best to use clay or other dense dirt.

Be sure that you keep the dirt at least four inches down from the siding though. If the siding is close or touching the soil, it will rot and you'll have another problem. Termites could also create a highway into your home undetected.

Don't rely on grading alone to keep your basement dry.

Gutters

Keep your gutters clean. There are a variety of gutter screening and cover materials that work well to keep them clean.

3

Downspouts

You didn't need to read a book to have someone tell you to keep your gutters from dumping water next to your foundation did you? I only have to say it so someone doesn't say my book is incomplete without this obvious advice.

So how do you do it. There are a few options to laying ugly pipes and contraptions across your lawn that get in the way of mowing and your annual croquet game at the family picnic.

One way is to bury pipes underground to the edge of the yard to take the roof water away. However, you need pitch on your yard to do it. And remember all the leaves and pine needles and acorns and twigs that wind up in your gutter will be going into those underground pipes and cause them to clog. If you do bury pipes underground I recommend you use as few elbows as possible and put as much pitch on the pipe as possible.

There are a few other options that work very well. A product called RainChute is recessed into the ground just an inch or so and takes the water up to 7 feet away. Usually this is all you need to make a big difference. The advantage of RainChute is that it is not above ground to cause a tripping or mowing problem and be unsightly,

Unsightly Tripping Hazard

RainChute

RainChute EZ

yet it is not underground either so it's not expensive and won't clog.

For areas that are landscaped and don't need mowing, a simple extension called RainChute EZ will do the trick.

"Curtain Drains" and Yard Drainage

The layman may suggest a "Curtain Drain" to cure your wet basement woes. Woah! This won't work.

A curtain drain is a trench in the ground some distance away from your foundation that has a pipe in it and is filled with crushed stone. Sometimes the trench will be filled to the top, appearing as a stripe of stone in your yard. This type of drain is often used on sloping lots on the uphill side of a building. It makes sense to intercept water coming down the hill, but can not be relied upon to prevent a basement from water problems.

Other types of shallow drains in a yard can only be relied upon to prevent puddling in the yard and not to prevent a basement from leaking. We have plenty of customers who drained their bank accounts with their local backhoe owner to no avail.

Stone River. *This "curtain drain" won't keep the basement dry.*

Insider Information

CAUTION

In and Out

Beware of waterproofing contractors who say they will do an outside AND inside drain. They tell you it's better because they stop the water from coming through your foundation – but why then do they need an inside system? Most customers are led to believe the outside drain will be very deep; and it seems to make sense. But in reality the installers just dig a trench 12" deep or so, and when they come to an obstacle like a porch or driveway they stop the trench and start again on the other side of the obstacle. The outside drain is useless.

The whole idea of a drain inside *and out* is window dressing to justify high prices for what they are providing.

Many people, including me, think it's a scam.

Chapter 4

Insider's Strategy

So if digging it up outside is not the answer, what is? Digging it up on the inside! Jackhammering to be more specific. By installing a drainage system around the inside of the basement along the wall, you can capture water at the most common point of entry – the floor/wall joint. You can also capture water from the walls and prevent the center of the floor from leaking by intercepting the water at the perimeter of the floor before it gets to the center.

The advantages of an interior drainage system include:

1. Accessibility to do the job.
2. More affordable than an outside system.
3. Installs in a day or two.
4. Easily serviceable year round.
5. It works.

Even in basements that are already finished, it's still much easier to waterproof from the inside than the outside. Most full-time basement waterproofing companies offer interior drainage systems – between which there are big differences in systems. Some are old fashioned and generic, and others are modern and specially designed for the job.

In the 1950's and before, clay pipe sections about 18 inches long were used for underground and under floor drains. There were no holes in the pipe, but instead the sections were laid with a ¼-inch space between them to let in water. Since the pipe sections were made from clay tile material – like a chimney flue pipe or a brick– they called it drain "tile." This term is still used today to refer to a pipe with holes or slots in it that is buried for drainage, even though the industry switched to plastic pipe long ago. These generic, round perforated drainpipes can be used for field drainage, exterior footing drains, road drainage, and just about anything.

Old fashioned - *clay "tile" pipe.*

Clay or plastic, the pipe was usually laid alongside the footing in new construction applications, and many contractors do the same for retrofitting an existing home. However, this placement of the pipe isn't necessarily the best. Existing drains alongside the footing have failed – usually by clogging with dirt. Slowly, different methods began to develop in the 60's, and afterwards. Today, a system called WaterGuard, developed in 1994, has proven to have all the benefits that homeowners and contractors are looking for.

WaterGuard is a specially-designed piping system engineered specifically to be a very efficient, long-lasting interior perimeter basement waterproofing system. The big difference is that the WaterGuard sits on top of the footing, instead of alongside the footing. This is important because the wet dirt (commonly referred to as Mud) can't get into the drain because the drain does not sit in the mud.

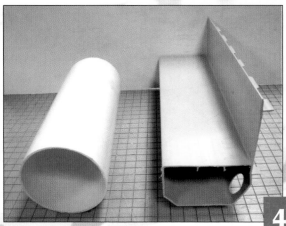

4

Which is for You? *Generic all-purpose drain pipe or WaterGuard, a specially designed piping system.*

Requirements of a good interior drainage system:

- ◆ Designed not to clog - sits on top of the footing
- ◆ Has a built in ⅜-inch gap between the floor and the wall to drain wall leaks
- ◆ Does not rely on filter fabric
- ◆ Has a big drain outlet to the sump
- ◆ Will not cause structural damage to the foundation

WaterGuard meets all these requirements. With a sub-floor system such as WaterGuard, an experienced installer can make various modifications to account for unusual foundation situations.

The Great Shape Debate

Some waterproofing companies make a big deal over the shape of their pipe. The fact is when you buy a drainage system you are not buying a pipe, but a space for water to flow in. The water doesn't care what shape the space is. The real question is _where_ the space is, and how it's set up to take water in and not mud.

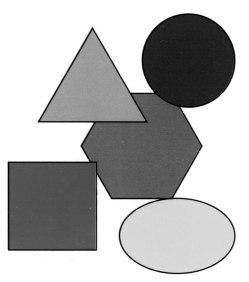

4

CAUTION

The Self-Flushing Lie

If anyone explains to you that their pipe is "self flushing", flush them from the competition to earn your business. To say such a thing implies that mud gets in but will be flushed out. Where did the mud come from? What's there after it gets "washed away" by the drainage system? Where does it go – into the sump hole to clog it up? Some contractors will take corrugated pipe (the cheapest of them all) and say the corrugations (which are not spirals) cause a spiraling action in the pipe to self-clean the pipe. This is a lie.

Another lie that's told sometimes is that parts of the floor must be left in place to prevent the walls from collapsing. If this were true, millions of homes would have fallen down by now.

Unfortunately the basement waterproofing industry has lots of characters who will say just about anything to make their pitch sound good to you and to down their competitors. Think about the statements that the salespeople are saying. If you smell a rat, there probably is one.

Deeper is Not Better

CAUTION

If a drainage system is too deep, it not only has a greater risk of clogging, but soil from underneath the foundation can wash into it and leave voids, which can cause settling of your foundation. Another issue is that you will be pumping out more water by trying to keep the water level much lower than necessary. Your pump could run all the time and the discharge water will keep the surface of your yard wet all the time.

The In-the-Mud Out-of-the-Mud Debate

Will all systems alongside the footing clog? No. But many will. Some soon, some later, some never. It depends on the soil and foundation conditions and the water problem. With the WaterGuard system, you never have to worry about the system clogging – and how many times do you want to have your basement waterproofed anyway?

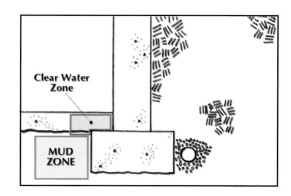

Clear Water Zone

MUD ZONE

Apples & Oranges

Up Above It. *Systems that sit in the mud can become part of the mud. Systems that sit above the mud will stay above it.*

Side Note

FIRE

The Alarmist?

I don't want to join the ranks of those who will tell you the sky will fall if you do something wrong. To my knowledge no basement waterproofer has ever killed a customer no matter what they did. The sun always comes up tomorrow. This is not life or death we're talking about. The worst that could happen is that you wind up paying a lot of money to have something fixed in your home and then some years later have the frustration of having to do parts of it or the whole thing over again. I don't want to sound like an alarmist with warnings of what not to do. It's your home and your money, and your decision. But since that's what this book is about, I am going to give you information to help eliminate the chances of your wasting any effort and money, and to get your WHOLE basement very dry, ALL the time.

4

The Floor/Wall Joint –
Open for Business

One important key to a waterproofing system is that it must have an opening to accept water from the walls. Wall leaks now or in the future include leaks from wall cracks, pipe penetrations, flooding window wells, condensation, and other miscellaneous sources. Of course we want to fix all of the leaks we see with the original installation, but we should also address new leaks that may come up in the future. A gap at the edge of the floor will catch any leaks, prevent the floor from getting wet, and prevent damage to anything that is on the floor.

This gap is sometimes called a "french drain," although those that know a little commonly use this term to mean different things. The gap along the wall can be made by sticking a piece of wood between the floor and wall, concreting up to it, and pulling it out. This makes a big ugly gap that can fill up with debris from the floor.

A better way is to have spacers along the backside of a flange that sticks up above the floor. $3/8$ inch is the optimum size for this gap. You want it to function and look nice and neat – as if it's supposed to be there.

Beware of systems that say they have a flange that is tight to the wall and yet takes water from the wall. If you have your 1st grade diploma, you know that's impossible.

Catch-All. *A french drain-style wall gap will catch water from the wall, as well as dirt and debris from the basement floor.*

4

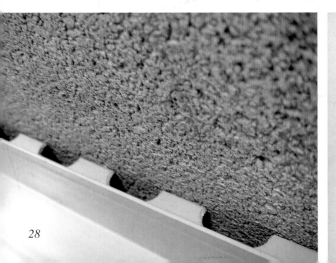

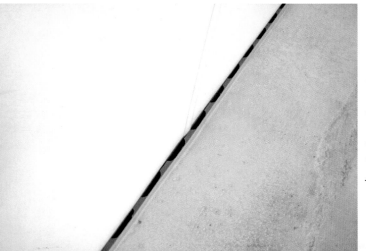

A Better Way. *WaterGuard flange spacers make a nice neat finished look and keep dirt and debris from the floor out of the gap.*

Monolithic Foundations
Require Special Care

A monolithic basement foundation is a two-piece foundation instead of a three piece one. The footing and floor are poured together in one shot, and then the walls are built on top of the floor. In other words, the floor is poured with thick edges to it and those thick edges are the footing.

In this case, it is not recommended to jackhammer the perimeter of the basement floor to install a sub floor perimeter drain system. It will take forever and be very dusty as well.

Instead, you should install an above-the-floor system called DryTrak, which does not require jackhammering the floor. DryTrak is a heavy vinyl baseboard system, which is permanently epoxied to the surface of the floor to channel water from the floor/wall joint and walls to the sump.

DRYTRAK™ COLLECTS AND CHANNELS WATER TO SUPERSUMP™

HYDROSTATIC PRESSURE IS RELIEVED WITH WEEPHOLES DRILLED THROUGH FLOOR

CONCRETE WALL EARTH

© Copyright 1994 Basement Systems, Inc.

PERMANENT SEAL

FOOTING

JOINT AND WEEPHOLES ALLOW WATER TO ENTER DRYTRAK™

It is a perfect solution for monolithic foundations.

If a contractor doesn't offer an above-floor system like DryTrak, he won't say anything when he encounters your monolithic foundation and either charge you a high price, or have his installers suffer through hammering away at it.

CAUTION

Beware of Filter Fabrics

Inside or outside, systems that use filter fabrics clog, slowing the flow rate down considerably. Think about the word "filter." What filter doesn't clog? And when it does how are you going to replace a filter under your basement floor?

4

Side
Note

Expect Dust

Like a patient who needs an operation, it gets worse before it gets better. But in the case of your home getting its water problem fixed, it only gets worse for a day or two.

Jackhammering in a home is loud – take the young and old out to the park the morning of the installation. It's also dusty. How dusty? Not very dusty at all if your basement floor is soft and damp. If your floor is hard and thick – you'll get more dust. Will that dust get upstairs? Maybe some will. On a windy day, it will. Plan on cleaning the house the day after the installation. In most homes it's not necessary.

Doorways and Stairways to the Outside

If you have a doorway or stairway that leads to the outside, you'll want to have a "trench drain" installed in front of it while you are having your waterproofing system installed. A trench drain is like a half round pipe with a grate that fits on top of it. The grate is flush or slightly below the floor to catch any water that may enter from the outside. It's easy to convert from WaterGuard along the perimeter of your basement floor to trench drain and back to WaterGuard again on the other side.

This way you are protected against leakage from a "hatchway door", a sliding door, or even a garage door. Even if your door doesn't leak now, with the right snow/ slush/ or heavy rain conditions it can. It doesn't cost any more to have the trench drain installed if your are having a WaterGuard system installed.

Radon Gas

Radon is a naturally occurring radioactive gas that comes from radium deposits in the earth's crust. If present in the soil under your home, it can get sucked into your house via the basement or crawl space.

Don't panic. It's fairly common and easy to get rid of.

Some people that know a little think that basement waterproofing and radon reduction systems are incompatible. While it's true that gaps, cracks, and holes in the basement floor and walls need to be sealed as part of the strategy to get rid of radon, this can be done without compromising the waterproofing system.

With products described in this book and a bit of extra caulk, your Basement Systems dealer can help you if your home has radon.

4

Clear Skies Ahead

Chapter 5

Up and Away
Sump Pumps – Better Than Ever

Now that you've channeled all groundwater that used to leak in from around the perimeter of your basement, you need to direct it to one spot and have some way of getting it out of your basement. You can either have a pipe that water flows through by gravity (downhill) to daylight, or use a sump pump to pump it up and out.

Gravity drains require that you have a substantial slope on your property so you can dig a trench from underneath your foundation to daylight while having the pipe pitch ⅛" per foot (one foot of pitch for every 100 feet you go out away from the house). Most homes don't have that kind of pitch on their property. And to get a trench that deep and go that far can be a big mess and cause substantial disturbance to other things outside your home. And remember your neighbors probably won't talk to you at this year's block party if you discharge it directly onto their property.

If gravity drains are easy to do on your property, it's not a bad option. But you must keep them from getting clogged, frozen or having the end covered over with ice or leaves and debris. I would recommend that a sump pump with an alarm be installed inside as a back up, so in case anything ever goes wrong with your gravity drain you can just plug the pump in.

For 99.9% of us, a sump pump is our best option. Despite any stories you have heard over the years about folks getting flooded because their sump pump was on the blink again, today's sump equipment is better than ever and very reliable – that is unless you cheap out and just buy a basic pump-in-a-hole. Then you'll be telling a tale of woe about your pump failing causing your basement to flood one day.

Pumps and Switches

When we say "sump", we mean the hole in the floor. The "pump" that goes in the sump is very important. There are different kinds of pumps that will perform differently and have shorter or longer expected lifetimes. I'll make it simple for you:

PUMPS

What is _not_ recommended .... Why

* Pedestal pumps that stick up above the floor .... You can't install them in an airtight sump, low capacity
* Plastic pumps .... They hold heat in and burn out faster, lower quality
* Pumps with screened inlets .... Screens clog easily, choking flow
* 1/4 hp pumps .... Too small

Automatic pump switches are vital too. The best pump in the world needs an excellent switch to tell it when to turn on and when to turn off.

SUMP PUMP SWITCHES

What is _not_ recommended .... Why

* "Ball on a wire" switches .... They need a big area to swing and can get hung up
* Pressure switches .... They aren't as precise and "on level" can change over time

PUMPS AND SWITCHES

What IS recommended .... Why

* Cast iron pumps .... Quiet, cool well, last long
* Mechanical float switches – float on a rod .... Reliable, positive on and off levels

Based on these criteria, I recommend Zoeller pumps. We have used them for years after brief stints with other pumps, and the results are very clear.

5

Pump, Don't Swirl

Many pump companies, and often their dealers, lie about how many gallons their pumps can pump to make them sound better than other manufacturers pumps. The most common way they get away with misleading folks like this is to quote how many gallons their pumps will move in an hour at a very low "head." Head is a term meaning how high you pump the water. So if you pump it 2 feet up out of the sump hole, and 7 feet over your basement wall, that's a 9 foot head. The higher the head, the lower the volume of water a pump can push.

Some pump companies quote how much water their pumps will pump at a 3-foot head. Who only has to pump water 3 feet high? This is totally irrelevant. Many even say "up to XXXX gallons per hour," when this number is at zero head! Who needs to pump water at zero head? The water is already there – you don't have to pump it! They should say, "will swirl water around a sump hole at 3500 gallons per hour." This is a misrepresentation of the highest order.

An AC pump that pumps over 2000 gallons per hour *at an 8 foot head* is a good strong pump.

The Pump is Only Part
of a Sump Pump System

Besides the pump, there are other elements of a good sump pump system that are very important.

The Sump Liner

You don't want your pump to clog up in a muddy hole in the floor. And you don't want it in a 5-gallon bucket that doesn't hold a lot of water and will cause the pump to "short cycle" (go on and off very quickly). Instead, you should have a sturdy liner or housing for your sump pump with holes in it to accept water directly from the ground as well as a larger inlet hole to allow your perimeter drainage system to empty into it. There should be about 100 $\frac{3}{8}$-inch holes in it. The liner should be about 2 feet deep and about 18 inches wide, and should have a rim that accepts a sealed cover.

Lifetime Warranty?

No pump manufacturer gives a lifetime warranty on their pumps – and there is a good reason why. A lifetime warranty doesn't make a pump better. Some irresponsible contractors will tell you there is a lifetime warranty (or many years) on their pump – "free replacements forever" – to seduce you to buy their whole solution. This is irresponsible. Ask yourself, "How do I know when to call to get my free replacement?" The answer is when your basement is flooded – and that's what this entire book is trying to prevent, as well as what you spent your money on in the first place to stop from happening. The damage will be done, and the 10 year, 20 year, or lifetime warranty won't help you.

! Airtight Sump Lid

Important

The sump should have an airtight lid on it to prevent water from evaporating out of the sump hole into your basement, to stop stuff from falling in that can clog the pump or switch, and to quiet the system. Depending on the cover, it can also make the installation look good too. Instead of a necessary evil in your home, you have a thought-fully engineered system.

All Too Common –

Low on performance and hard on the eyes.

It doesn't have to be this way...

FORM & FUNCTION

A Sump Pump as Art

A Floor Drain in the Sump Lid

Not *if*, but *when* you have a plumbing leak and the water floods out onto the basement floor, you'll want to use your sump hole to drain the water away. With an airtight lid, the water will fill up your basement. (Unlike groundwater leaks, plumbing leaks and the damage they cause might be covered by your homeowner's insurance.) Putting a floor drain in the sump lid is the answer. But wait, won't a sump drain allow water vapor to evaporate into my basement? Not with Basement Systems' airtight floor drain. This places a specially designed cup and ball underneath the floor drain which allows water to go down, but doesn't allow air to come up.

Important

A Stand for the Pump

A "CleanPump Stand" will elevate the pump off the bottom of the sump liner a bit, allowing for some sediment, mud, debris, or gravel that washes into the sump liner to settle to the bottom of the sump liner without clogging or otherwise affecting the pump. It also keeps the check valve and discharge pipe clean. A check valve (one-way valve) should be installed on all sump pump discharge lines, so when the pump shuts off the water in the pipe doesn't flow back into the sump hole, which would then have to be pumped again on the next cycle.

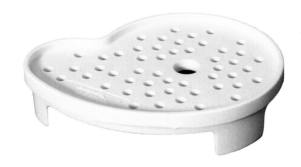

Important

Pump Alarms

How would you know if your sump pump has failed and you were in danger of being flooded? Unless you have an alarm, the answer is, when your basement is already flooded, which is just what you are trying to avoid. A battery powered alarm that sounds off automatically when the water reaches a level above the point where the pump(s) should normally turn on is essential. The patented WaterWatch alarm does just that, telling you there is a problem before the floor gets wet, so you have a chance to do something about it.

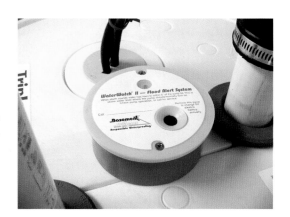

This is a **BIG** IDEA!

Important for **Finished Basements**

What if my pump fails?
What if the power goes out?

These are questions you should be asking yourself. After all, you want your WHOLE basement dry ALL the time, right? Well, you're not going to get that if you don't plan on...

❖ The power going out one day – which usually happens in a big storm with rain
❖ The pump coming unplugged
❖ The circuit breaker tripping
❖ The primary pump failing
❖ The primary pump not being able to keep up with the amount of water in a very heavy rain

5

Remember all the stories of woe people have told you about the sump pump failing and them getting flooded? These are the reasons they were talking about. You don't have to go through that if you get the right equipment.

AC/DC

AC = (Alternating Current) plugged into the wall – runs off house power

DC = (Direct Current) Runs off battery power

Side Note

1+1=1

If you have more than one AC pump to get more water out in a big rain, it makes no sense to hook them up to one discharge pipe. Using the "Ten pounds of stuff in a five pound bag" logic, you can't get more water out with two pumps unless you have two discharge pipes to the outside.

The King (and Queens) of Sump Pumps

The answer is a system called the "TripleSafe" sump pump system. This top-of-the-line system sports three sump pumps in one sump liner. Pump 1 is a high-quality Zoeller $^1/_3$ hp pump and will do the lions share of the pumping very efficiently most of the time.

Pump two is a $^1/_2$ hp Zoeller pump set a bit higher in the sump hole that turns on in the event that the first pump can't keep up or if it fails. This second pump is more powerful and has a separate discharge line to give you that "turbo boost" in those rare cases that you need it.

Pump 3 is an "UltraSump," DC (battery operated) pump that kicks in if the power goes out. It is available with one or two specially designed batteries to pump out over 8000 or over 16,000 gallons of water respectively at an 8-foot head.

The TripleSafe twin liner, lids, CleanPump Stands, bridge, etc., are all specially engineered to work together.

3
Pump 3-UltraSump® Battery Back-up Pumping System
(Battery and automatic charging system are included)

1
Pump 1-Zoeller M-53
1/3 hp Pump

Pump 2-
Zoeller M-98
1/2 hp High
Volume Pump

2

Pump 3 operating range

Pump 2 operating range

Pump 1 operating range

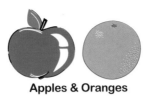

Insider
Information

Finished
Basements

Apples & Oranges

Importance of a Backup Pumping System

It is important to note that there are many kinds of "back-up" systems provided. I just saw one with a contractor price of $79, which he would put together with a $50 car battery and sell for $400 to $800. When it comes to back-up equipment, the variance of quality is a chasm. The low-end equipment most often will not work when you need it. And the folks like you who buy back-up pumping equipment really need and want the protection.

To give you an example, nearly all suppliers of back-up equipment do not supply batteries. Batteries are heavy and expensive and difficult to ship. Instead, they leave it to the contractor to go to the automotive store and buy a car battery. Car batteries are not made for this application. Their ampere-hour capacity diminishes quickly after a year in this application and will not get the "gallonage" out of your basement when you need it to.

Float switches are extremely important too. The best pump in the world needs to have a switch to tell it when to go on and off. Many primary and back-up pump systems come with a tethered float switch – a "ball-on-a-wire" design. These have to swing up and down to operate and commonly get hung up – and cause a flood.

No pump or back-up pump is perfect. But so many are really pitiful protection. That's why Basement Systems TripleSafe and UltraSump are specifically engineered to do what we need them to, and offer redundancy.

5

Hey, We'll Throw 4 Pumps in the Sump Hole

Trade Secrets

Insider Information

You can't just throw a bunch of pumps in the floor and expect great results. The "bull in a China shop" approach to improving on a TripleSafe system (no improvement necessary) is to cram as many pumps into the floor as you can – 4 are better than 3, right? Wrong!

Engineers attended to every detail of the TripleSafe system. It's all you need!

Car batteries are for... well... cars. They don't work very well on back-up sump systems.

Side Note

Is a Generator an Option?

A generator is a good idea if you have an automatic one permanently installed that senses when the power goes out and starts up automatically. It needs to be wired by an electrician. A typical generator can be hooked up to run your sump pump, a few lights, the furnace, and the fridge. This costs between $7,000 to $10,000 in most cases. If you go this route, be sure to install two AC primary pumps to cover you in case of pump failure, as a generator only eliminates the need for the DC back-up pump.

You can purchase a portable generator for $400 or so. However you have to be home (and awake) to notice when the power fails. Then you have to drag the generator outside, gas it up, start it up, and run an extension cord to your sump pump. This is not a good option.

How to Figure How Much Battery Back-up Protection You are Buying

Trade Secrets
Insider Information

A simple equation can tell you how many gallons your equipment can pump out of your basement when the power goes out.

Gallons out = Ampere-hour capacity of the battery / DC amps of the pump x Gallons per hour rating of the pump at 8 feet high.

In the case of Basement Systems UltraSump:

Gal. out = Amp hour of battery /DC amps of pump x gph

Gal. out = 90 / 15.5 x 1500

Gal. out = 5.806 x 1500

Gal. out = 8709

This calculation assumes you are pumping the water 8 feet high and that the battery is new. As batteries age, they lose some of their ampere hour capacity. Because of these and other factors, we usually understate the performance.

A special unit called an UltraSump Dual Battery Switching Unit allows two batteries to be hooked up, doubling the number of gallons the back-up pump will pump out.

Everyone asks "How long will the pump last?" We can't answer this question because it is the wrong question. How long your battery back-up pump will last in a power outage depends upon how hard it rains when the power is out and how much water is in the ground under your particular home. One thing is for sure, 8000 gallons of water is a lot of water.

An Entire Pool? *Can an Ultra-Sump with a 100 amp battery pump out a 9000-gallon swimming pool at an 8' head?*

You betcha! *On a single battery, the UltraSump emptied the pool and was raring to attack the pond in back.*

Alternate Power

CAUTION

Some alternate power sources for sump pumps appeared on the market in recent years that sound great at first review. One is a battery power system for your primary AC operated pump. When the power goes out the system converts the DC power to AC power and runs your only sump pump. The manufacturer will tell you that it's better since your primary AC operated pump will normally pump more than a DC operated one. This is true, but not a key issue in most cases. The main issue or problem here is that you have only one pump. If the pump fails you get flooded despite this back-up protection. Secondly, converting DC to AC power is very inefficient. You lose more than half your power in the process. So your primary pump will run and pump plenty of water out, but not for long. In our test it was only one hour of time and then the batteries went dead. Since the primary pump we used pumped 2200 gallons an hour, it was just 2200 gallons of protection this system offered.

The next type of system that sounds good is another single-pump system that can be used as a primary and back-up pump in one unit. It is actually a DC pump with batteries hooked up to it. When the power is on the AC is converted to DC to run the pump. When the power is off the pump runs on the batteries. Sounds good. But you only have one pump and if it fails your dead in the water. In addition, no matter how strong the DC pump, you only get as much water out equal to the amount of battery power you put behind the pumps.

Side Note

Electrical Outlets

Electrical Outlet(s) are usually not included in the scope of work by your waterproofing contractor. Although your waterproofer will leave with your sumps operational, plan on having a electrician wire a proper outlet at the sump location after the waterproofer is done.

5

If it doesn't snow in the winter where you are, skip this.

Important

Freezing Discharge Lines

Your sump pump gets the water out of the basement and away from your house with a pipe – usually plastic and usually about 1½ inches in diameter. This pipe runs on the surface of the ground or in a shallow buried trench and discharges the water onto the surface away from the house.

The problem is that in winter the outlet of the pipe becomes blocked with snow and ice. When the pump runs, it fills the pipe with water. (Ten feet of 1½-inch pipe holds one gallon of water). Since the water can't get out of the pipe due to the ice at the outlet, the whole pipe fills with water and freezes. Now your pump runs, but cannot get the water out, and your basement floods. Just what you were trying to avoid!

Basement Systems has a solution – The IceGuard system. This is a specially engineered fitting that goes outside your home and automatically ejects the water away from the exterior wall in the event that the pipe freezes. It is designed with holes in it to allow this to happen, yet no water at all gets out of these openings when the pipe is not frozen.

Snow, no problem. *The patented IceGuard solves the problem of frozen discharge lines.*

With a TripleSafe pump system, both discharge lines are protected by the IceGuard sump pump discharge line system.

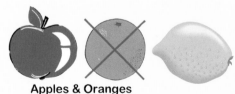

Apples & Oranges

Insider Information

A Real Dog

Beware of some contractors who use a roof drain contraption with slots all the way around, and try to pass it off as such a device. Because water dribbles along the slots (spilling next to the foundation) when the pump runs, the fitting freezes up and closes off the escape openings.

A lot of discussion about sump pumps and pump related issues – right? Well – you said you wanted your basement dry ALL the time!

The short answer is to get a TripleSafe sump pump system with two discharge lines protected by the IceGuard sump pump discharge line system...

...NOW *you're safe*

Why didn't I just tell you that first?

Chapter 6

Upright Remedies
How to Heal Your Damp, Ugly Basement Walls

Once you have drained water away at the perimeter of your basement floor, and made sure it's pumped out reliably, the next thing you'll want to think about is your basement walls. You can get your basement floor dry without doing anything to your basement walls – but is that what you want?

Your basement walls allow water vapor to pass through them. Block walls not only allow lots of water vapor through because of their hollow core, but cold (and damp) outside air passes through them easily. And air, water, and water vapor can pass through stone walls.

Take a look at your basement walls. Chances are they are damp, stained, chalky, flaky, and ugly. Ask yourself if you are happy with them. Chances are the answer is no. So what can you have done?

There are a few options including coatings, paneling, and vapor barriers.

Wall Coatings

Coatings are not a good option simply because they don't stay on the wall for a very long time. This is because the water and water vapor are already through the wall by the time they get to the coatings and push the coating off the wall. When they begin to peel and flake, the wall looks worse than it did in the first place.

3 Good Options

There are three good options for what do to with your basement walls. Choosing the best one depends upon what you are doing with your basement.

If you –

❖ Are leaving your basement unfinished – then "BrightWall" paneling is best

❖ Are finishing your basement – then "ThermalDry Wall System" is best

❖ Have stone walls – Then "CleanSpace" is best for unfinished basements or ThermalDry Wall System is best if you are finishing it.

You'll Love This!

BrightWall Paneling

Think of it as a plastic version of Formica. BrightWall is semi-rigid white plastic panels that get installed on your basement walls with drilled-in white fasteners. It can never come off of your walls no matter how much dampness comes through.

BrightWall paneling drains any water leaks down behind it to the (WaterGuard) perimeter drainage system without you ever knowing it. It also stops water vapor from coming through the walls and evaporating into your basement.

Most of all it really dresses up your unfinished basement! BrightWall looks great and makes the basement much brighter with the available lighting down there.

Like plastic Formica. *BrightWall paneling system stops water vapor from permeating through basement walls and drains water down to a perimeter drainage system (WaterGuard) if necessary. Plus, it looks great and really brightens a basement!*

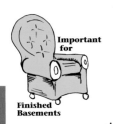

ThermalDry WALL System

ThermalDry Wall System is part of a likely pair of products for folks who are finishing their basements, along with ThermalDry Floor Matting. The Wall system, a plastic vapor barrier with bubbles on one side that act as thermal breaks and spacers to allow for drainage, stops water vapor from getting into your basement through the walls and drains water from any wall leaks to the drainage system below.

More than that, because of its reflective foil face, the ThermalDry Wall system reflects more than 90% of the heat from your basement back into the basement, providing energy savings. Heat moves from hot to cold, and your basement walls are always cold because the earth is cold. Normally the thermal mass of your basement walls perpetually soaks up heat from your home. With the ThermalDry Wall System in between, this process dramatically slows down, saving energy.

Mechanically fastened with drilled-in fasteners, ThermalDry Wall System is perfect for people who are going to cover their basement walls with a stud wall in the future.

Is it good for unfinished basements? If you don't mind the look, sure. However it is not as durable as BrightWall and can rip if abused.

3-in-1. *ThermalDry WALL system stops water vapor, drains wall leaks, and reflects heat back into your basement – the perfect solution before finishing your basement!*

CleanSpace Wall System

We use CleanSpace, a heavy, durable plastic liner – like a pool liner, for lining dirt crawl spaces. It is perfect as a wall solution for stone wall basements. Because stone walls are not flat, they are not candidates for BrightWall paneling. The CleanSpace provides a vapor barrier, drains water behind it, and dramatically brightens the basement. It will have little waves in it because it comes off of a roll rather than in panels, but the CleanSpace is very durable and nearly impossible to rip.

The solution to damp and leaking stone walls.
CleanSpace Wall system stops water vapor, drains wall leaks, and brightens your basement – especially effective in basements with stone walls.

What's that White Chalky Powder?

Efflorescence is from minerals in the concrete, mortar, or soil that dissolve in water and remain behind when the water evaporates off the surface of the wall or floor. It appears as white powder or crystals. It is sometimes confused with mold, but it is not alive – just mineral residue. It is not harmful and can be swept or brushed off. It is a sign that water is (probably, slowly) coming through the wall or floor.

Thinking of Coating or Painting Your Walls?

Think again. Coating basement walls or floors accomplishes nothing except to make them look better. However they will only look better until the paint or coating starts to peel, and then they look much worse. I'd say don't bother.

Will Mold Grow Behind BrightWall, CleanSpace, or ThermalDry Wall?

Not unless your walls are painted with latex paint or are very dirty. Mold needs organic material such as wood, paper, or cardboard on which to grow. It will not grow on clean, wet concrete or plastic, unless there is dirt on the surface. In this case, the mold is growing on the dirt, not on the concrete or plastic. (Latex is rubber from trees, and therefore organic).

To keep mold from growing we need to keep organic materials dry. Inorganic materials such as plastic, glass, concrete, metal, etc., should be installed in places we can't keep dry.

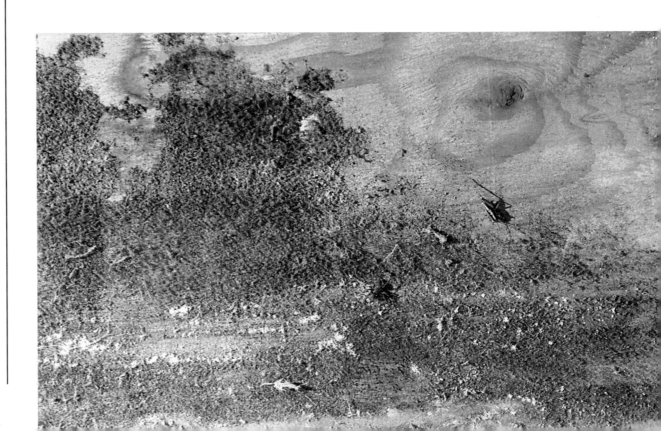

Which is for You?

Before

Unfinished concrete walls are cold, damp, and uninviting.

After With BrightWall®

Completing walls with BrightWall® Paneling brightens your basement and gives it that clean finished touch.

After With ThermalDry® Wall

Using the ThermalDry® Wall System to cover your basement walls helps to insulate your home, reflecting over 90% of the heat back in.

After With CleanSpace®

Covering your basement walls with the CleanSpace® Wall System economically brightens your basement.

All 3 Systems drain wall leaks to a waterproofing system below, and stop water vapor from coming through the walls.

While any of the three wall systems are appropriate in dry basements, if there is ground water seepage, before or after the installation, our WaterGuard or DryTrak systems (discussed in Chapter 4) should be installed to control the water.

Chapter 7

Your Basement Floor
Making it Suitable for Carpet

Important for

Finished Basements

To most people who have had a series of unsettling wet basement episodes, the idea of laying a carpet and using that part of the house as finished space is one that would never seem possible. But think about it now. So far we have prevented the whole basement floor from getting wet with a WaterGuard system around the full perimeter of the basement and we have kept it that way with a TripleSafe sump pump system. Then we made the walls nice and dry with one of the wall systems. So now we don't have a wet basement floor – we have a damp one instead.

Damp floor! Now hold the phone you say! What do you mean damp?

Well, we have controlled the groundwater leakage, but there is another much slower way moisture can move into our space. Water vapor can pass through the floor slab, because concrete is porous and the ground is damp. In newer homes built by good builders who care, there may be a plastic vapor barrier under the floor, installed before the floor was poured. This means, you probably don't have one. In fact, we almost never encounter a vapor barrier under a floor when installing sump pump systems.

Water vapor passing through a slab is a slow process. As moisture passes through, it evaporates off the surface of the basement floor, so the floor doesn't appear wet. However, if we install a carpet on top of the slab, the carpeting slows the evaporation process down, and the moisture builds up in the carpeting.

The high relative humidity in the carpeting causes mold to grow, which causes that musty smell that makes basement spaces so unpleasant. Besides that, it can rot the carpet, causing premature replacement. And anyone allergic to mold is not going to be a happy camper in the basement.

For us earth dwellers, the floor is the surface of a room that we are in constant contact with. Carpet laid over hard, cold, damp concrete doesn't feel as comfortable as carpet on a softer, warmer, and completely dry subfloor.

So what can you do?

The old fashioned, "I-had-no-other-choice" option is to lay a wood floor down and put carpet on that. This sounds good – until the wood floor starts to rot and smell. And who has 3 or 4 inches of headroom to lose in a basement?

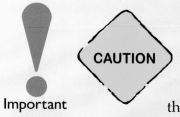

The biggest problem with wood subfloors, or any floor in a basement that involves wood, is that one day you will have to replace the floor when it gets wet from a plumbing leak. (I am assuming you have opted to go with the TripleSafe sump pump system. If not, add pump failure to plumbing leaks as the tragic events that WILL happen and make your life miserable for a month or so, and leave you poorer for it.)

Your basement is a big hole under a structure you call your home. Your home is full of pipes. Drain pipes and pressurized supply pipes. You also have tubs, toilets, showers, dishwashers, a refrigerator with a water line to it for ice and water, and sinks. If (I should say "when") something goes wrong, and water leaks, overflows, bursts, or otherwise escapes out of this plumbing system, where do you think it will wind up?

(Hint – Remember Janesky's First Law of Hydrodynamics – Water flows downhill.)

Right – in the basement. So, now you have a wooden subfloor invariably made of plywood or chipboard that is soaked through, top and bottom, with the carpet, like a wet sponge, laying on it. Typically this subfloor remains wet for a long time because you can't get the water out from under the subfloor. Unless... You guessed it.

You rip up the carpet and rip up the wood subfloor and start over. Hopefully the stud walls are not built on top of the wood subfloor, then you'll have to…oh…trust me – **Important** – NO WOOD SUBFLOORS IN BASEMENTS!

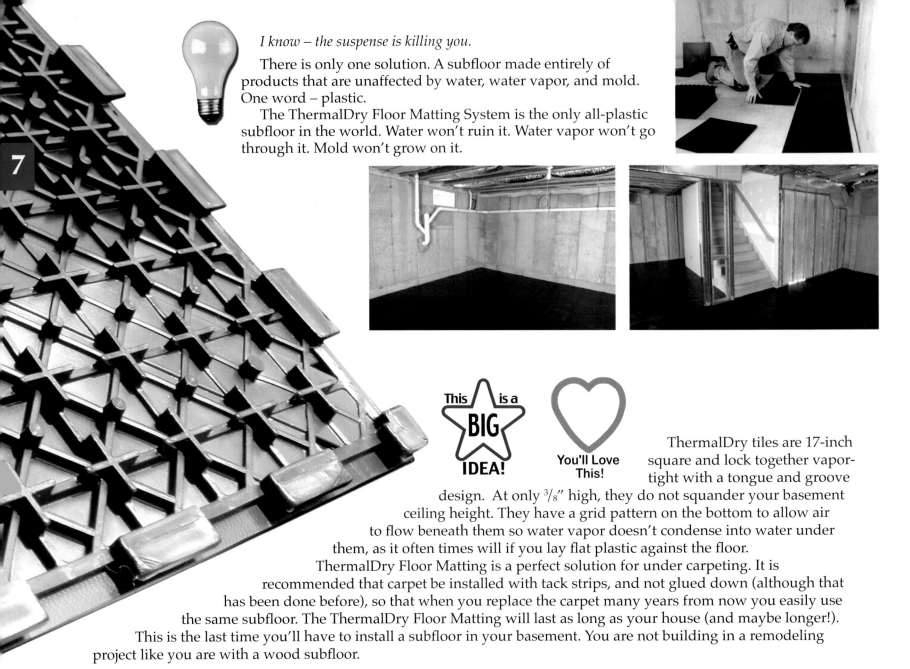

I know – the suspense is killing you.

There is only one solution. A subfloor made entirely of products that are unaffected by water, water vapor, and mold. One word – plastic.

The ThermalDry Floor Matting System is the only all-plastic subfloor in the world. Water won't ruin it. Water vapor won't go through it. Mold won't grow on it.

This is a BIG IDEA!

You'll Love This!

ThermalDry tiles are 17-inch square and lock together vapor-tight with a tongue and groove design. At only ³/₈" high, they do not squander your basement ceiling height. They have a grid pattern on the bottom to allow air to flow beneath them so water vapor doesn't condense into water under them, as it often times will if you lay flat plastic against the floor.

ThermalDry Floor Matting is a perfect solution for under carpeting. It is recommended that carpet be installed with tack strips, and not glued down (although that has been done before), so that when you replace the carpet many years from now you easily use the same subfloor. The ThermalDry Floor Matting will last as long as your house (and maybe longer!). This is the last time you'll have to install a subfloor in your basement. You are not building in a remodeling project like you are with a wood subfloor.

The ThermalDry Floor Matting system keeps your carpeted floor dry, warmer, and more comfortable while making your carpet last up to twice as long as it would otherwise.

Apples & Oranges

CAUTION

Wood + Water = Bad

Subfloor tiles available at big box stores made of chipboard with dimpled plastic material on the bottom are a disaster waiting to happen. Not only does the wood floor get wet, but the plastic dimples beneath are facing up and fill with water in the event of a plumbing leak, sealing your floors doom.

Repeat after me – Wood plus Water equals BAD! Forget the wood on a basement floor.

Important

A Hardwood Basement?

Wood-finished floors are not recommended in basements for the same reasons wood subfloors are not. Get rid of your visions of hardwood or parquet floors in your basement. Bad idea. Bad. (Unless you enjoy the process of *replacing* wood floors – then I'd say go for it.)

Mold & Fungus Heaven!

"Carpenter Ready"

Carpenters don't know what to do with a basement floor. To be fair, most waterproofing contractors don't know about carpentry either. The time to take care of the floor and make it "Carpenter Ready" is when you have a knowledgeable waterproofing contractor who offers Thermal-Dry Floor Matting.

Ahhh, plastic. When it comes to making basements mold-free usable space I don't know what we'd do without plastic. Polypropylene, polyethylene, PVC, polystyrene, ABS – mold is just not interested.

You Want a Dry Basement, Not a Shorter One

ThermalDry Floor Matting only takes up $3/8$" of your ceiling height. Good news for tall folks.

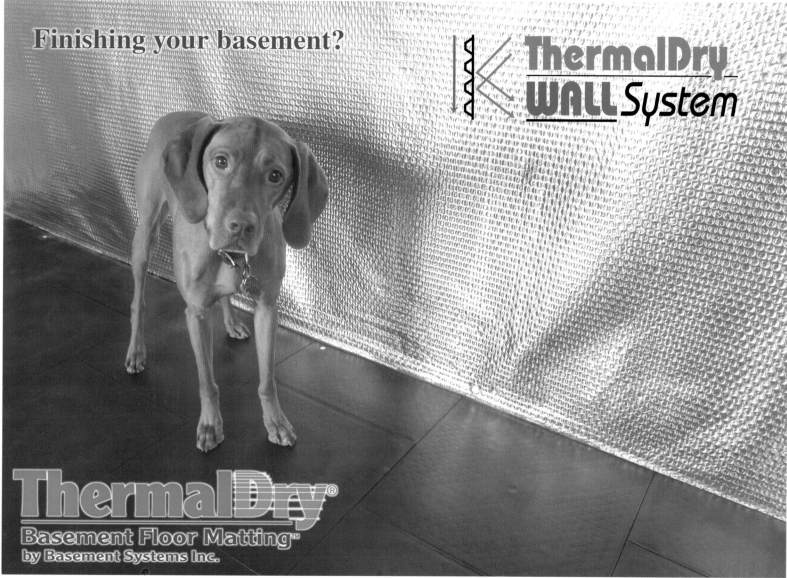

Finishing your basement?

ThermalDry WALL System

ThermalDry®
Basement Floor Matting™
by Basement Systems Inc.

The ThermalDry System creates a thermal break at the cold, damp concrete walls and floor, and prevents water vapor from permeating through the concrete into your basement space.

Chapter 8

Mastering Humidity
The Anti-Mold

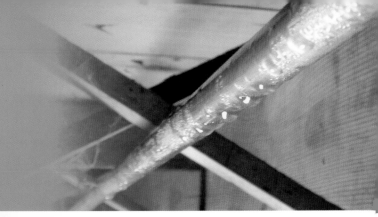

When "dry" means – feels dry, smells dry, and looks dry.

Just because you have a waterproofing system, doesn't mean you have a dry basement. There I go again with the confusing statement. Bear with me, because this is important.

There are 4 ways basements become wet or damp.

1. Groundwater leakage. (We have this one taken care of in the chapters we've covered so far).

2. Capillary action. Meaning wicking. For example a block wall may not leak, but it feels damp because it's wicking the water inside it to the surface like a sponge.

3. Water vapor coming through your walls and floor. (By installing one of the wall systems and our ThermalDry Floor Matting, we don't have to worry about wicking and have slowed water vapor transmission down considerably.)

4. The last way water gets into your basement is from exterior air leaking into your basement. This is not a problem as long as the outside air is cooler than the basement. It's the warmer summertime air that moves lots of water into our basement.

This is a **BIG** IDEA!

Whenever the outside air is warmer than the inside air, and especially when it's humid outside air, we are likely to have a condensation problem in our subterranean levels. This is because the Relative Humidity of air goes up 2.2% for every one-degree you cool it. Our basements are always cool because they are below ground. And we know that a house is like a chimney – air flows upwards, allowing air to escape the upper levels, with new make-up air being sucked in at the lower levels.

So when it's hot and humid in the summer, rain or not, our basement may be the wettest it has been all year!

If it's an 80-degree day with Relative Humidity of 80%, and we suck this air into our basements and cool it to 68 degrees, the Relative Humidity goes up by 26.4% (12 degrees x 2.2%). But wait a minute, 80% plus 26.4% is more than 100%, and we can't have more than 100%. So instead, as the air becomes saturated it gives up its moisture on your cold basement walls, floor, water tank, pipes, and other cold things. This is called condensation.

Even without condensation, we still get high relative humidity levels, which allows mold to grow and cause "stinky basement syndrome." And dust mites are having a party. More on that later.

In order to eliminate condensation you need to either heat the air (ridiculous in summer), or take water out of it (easy to do). Correction. I should say take water out of it *efficiently and effectively* (not so easy unless you have the right equipment to do it with).

8

Not Just on Concrete. *Condensation can form on cold water pipes and ducts too.*

You'll *really* Love This!

Not Just Any Dehumidifier

A dehumidifier is the plain answer. But not just any dehumidifier. I have been dealing with this issue intensely for nearly 20 years. The only machine that will get you the results you need is one called a SaniDry Basement Air System. And it's awesome.

The SaniDry is a high-capacity, high-efficiency dehumidification system, with air filtration, in a single unit. The SaniDry takes up to 100 pints of water per day out of your basement air, while using the same energy as a "40 pint" dehumidifier. And it filters particles out of the air to less than an incredible two microns in size – which is smaller than any mold spore or dust mite dropping.

The SaniDry Basement Air System wrings your air dry, and its powerful blower moves that dry air out into and around your basement space. This dry air then dries your building materials and basement contents, which makes the damp smell and damp feeling go away! What a huge difference a SaniDry can make in "condensation season." People really love their dry basement environments after having a SaniDry installed.

You'll also never have to empty any buckets on your SaniDry system because it automatically drains into your WaterGuard system or sump.

Having a groundwater-free basement is one thing. Adding a SaniDry is like putting the cherry on top of your dry basement program. It makes it complete. I haven't seen many basements that <u>don't</u> need one. Picture the concrete in your basement turning white because it is so dry!

8

How does it perform so incredibly well with the same amount of energy that less-effective 20-pound-weakling dehumidifiers use?

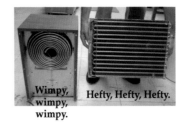

Wimpy, wimpy, wimpy.　Hefty, Hefty, Hefty.

1. The SaniDry blows air over a huge cold coil. It looks like a truck radiator instead of the little squirrelly spiral coil of dinky dehumidifiers.

2. The SaniDry runs the exiting dry cold air through a special heat-exchange core that pre-cools the incoming wet air and recaptures energy.

3. The SaniDry's powerful 200 cfm blower not only grabs more air in to dry faster, but moves the dry air out around your basement to dry the contents of your basement.

Powerful blower. *200 cfm blower really moves dehumidified air around to dry the entire space.*

You'd Never Keep Up. *The SaniDry drains to a sump pump, WaterGuard system, or directly outside so you never have to empty a bucket again – there's no option to even do so as you'd be bailing all day and night.*

There are other component reasons SaniDry wins the dehumidifier battle, but these are the main ones.

To further prove its mettle, SaniDry is Energy Star rated – a rare achievement for a dehumidification system.

Another big benefit of the SaniDry system is that it doesn't have to be located in the space it's drying. You can locate it in a utility room and duct the wet air in and dry air out to the main room of your basement.

With no water leaks and dry air, materials stay dry and you can finish your basement or use it for storage.
No smell, no mold, no property damage.

Did I mention I  love the SaniDry system? And you will too.

Why Household Dehumidifiers Just Don't Do the Job

1. They are too small.

2. The cold coil (the actual thing that takes the water out of the air) is too small.

3. The fan is too small (it has to be so it doesn't blow the air past the dinky coil too fast, otherwise it wouldn't take <u>any</u> water out!)

4. The fan doesn't circulate the dry air around your basement – because it's too small.

5. They usually aren't drained automatically, so the bucket fills up and they shut off.

6. They are rated (25 pints, 30 pints, 40 pints, etc.) per day at 80 degrees air temperature. Warm air holds a lot more moisture than cold air. Put them in a 68 degree basement and their effectiveness goes way down below this number.

There is simply no comparison between a SaniDry Basement Air System and any dehumidifier you've ever seen. I am usually a bit conservative and always realistic about what a product can do. The SaniDry Basement Air System is one product where I let all the performance promises hang out.

Open Sump Hole?

Having an open sump hole and running a dehumidifier is like trying to fill a bucket with a hole in it. As you dry the air, more water evaporates into it via the open sump hole with a pool of water sitting in it all year. In other words you have a dehumidifier and a humidifier.

8

Dehumidifiers Should Drain Automatically

Quick –

How many hours in a week? **168**.

How long would it take a cheapo dehumidifier's bucket to fill up and shut off? **Maybe 12**.

If you empty it once a week, what percentage of the time is it actually running? If you're not a mathlete, the answer is **7% of the time**. Meaning it's <u>off</u> for 93% of the time.

Who wants to have "Empty dehumidifier bucket" on their daily chore sheet? The answer is to hook it up with a hose to **automatically drain the water away** – and you never have to empty it.

What Makes a Basement Smell Like One?

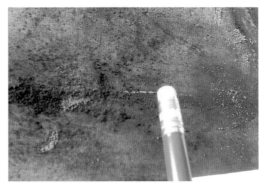

Answer = Mold.

Mold can grow in a "waterproofed basement."

Mold needs organic material to grow (which you have), and high relative humidity – over 60 to 70%. It doesn't have to be wet for mold to grow, just humid. In fact, mold won't grow underwater.

A SaniDry Basement Air System ensures that the relative humidity stays below 50% all year long so mold doesn't have a chance.

There are a lot of mold experts. But one that tells you to eliminate the mold without eliminating the water and humidity is not helping you. Some tell you to coat your floor joists and other structural elements with anti-mold paint.

To me, this is to say that if it's humid and mold wants to grow, the paint will stop it from growing. Assuming that's true, what about the contents of your basement? If you have a cardboard box, does it have to be painted too? How about your sofa? Call me crazy, but if it's really dry down there with low humidity, mold won't grow with or without a coating.

(I'm not crazy, that's the way it works.)

Save Money
Dry Air is Easier to Cool!

Damp indoor air costs more money to cool. Sure, a SaniDry costs a bit in electricity to run, but lower cooling costs in part offset this electric cost. This is because your central air system has to remove the moisture from the air in order to cool it, and that takes energy. Air conditioning systems are inefficient at dehumidifying.

If you dry the air in your basement, that air rises into the rest of the house, making the whole house drier.

Apples & Oranges

SaniDry – Energy Test Winner!

We tested four dehumidifiers to find out the cost per pint of water removed from the air. The worst performer was a standard household unit available under any number of recognizable brand names. It came out at more than 11 cents per pint removed. A higher priced unit, but one without the features of the SaniDry, costed about 10 cents per pint of water removed. The big winner was the SaniDry, which costed only 3.3 cents per pint of water removed! What a bargain!

Dust Mites – #1 Indoor Allergen

The number one thing that people with asthma and allergies react to indoors is dust mite droppings. These parasites live in your furniture, bedding, and carpeting, and feed off dead skin flakes. Their droppings are so small that they become airborne, are breathed in, and thus can irritate humans. Dust mites need relative humidity above 50% to live, as they absorb water out of the air rather than drinking it. Therefore, dry the air and dust mites die.

We have heard of a story of a doctor in West Virginia prescribing a SaniDry unit on his prescription pad! Now there's an enlightened doctor!

For more information go to www.housedustmite.com

Fan-in-a-Box
Too Good to be True

Some waterproofing contractors offer another unit that debuted on the market around 2003. Truth be told, most of these contractors do not even understand why the unit is a bad idea, and just go by the manufacturer's specifications. The unit consists of a fan in a tall sheet metal cabinet with a humidistat on it and an exhaust duct to the outside, like a dryer vent. The way it's supposed to work is when the humidity gets high the fan automatically turns on and sucks air off of the basement floor and exhausts it outside. New make-up air is supposed to come down from upstairs where it's drier – so it's supposed to dry your basement.

The idea, they say, is that wet air is heavier than dry air, so if you suck air out of your house from near the basement floor, you are exhausting the wettest air. The problem is that it's not true. Warm air holds a lot more water than cold air, and everyone knows that warm air rises. The reason there is more humidity in the basement as previously noted, is that the basement is cold, and when air is cooled the relative humidity goes up unless we remove water from the air.

The problem with exhausting air out of your house is that it is indoor conditioned air – you paid to cool it, heat it, and in the process dehumidify it via your HVAC system. If you exhaust this air out, then new air has to come in to replace it. Where does the new air come from? Outside of course. And unless it's a perfect day outside – like 70 degrees and 50% relative humidity, outside air needs to be heated or cooled, and dehumidified to be comfortable, and that costs money.

Heat it, Cool it, then Blow it Outside?
The fan-in-a-box dehumidifier exhausts your conditioned air, and your money.

The brochures on these "fan-in-a-box" units explain that the units only cost pennies in electricity to run. That's true. But it costs a lot more than that in air conditioning and heating bills, which you are probably not going to associate with this unit. Everyone is aware of energy saving things to do like caulking, weather-stripping, insulating, and installing tighter windows and doors. Why would you put a fan to blow air out of (and suck air into) your home on purpose? (There are other issues regarding ventilation but most homes are so leaky…well, that's a whole 'nuther book.)

You've already invested money in your indoor air,
so stick with it and dehumidify it.

Keep Basement Windows Closed!

There is no reason to open a basement window for any type of climate control. When the air outside is cooler than inside you loose heat. When it's warmer outside you bring in moisture. Keep basement windows closed.

O *ur newly configured and different-looking SaniDry CSB model is a great new offering for crawl space and basement dehumidification. Your dealer will pick the right model for you – you really can't go wrong.*

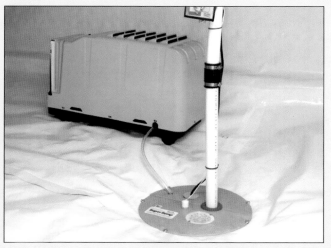

8

Chapter 9

Window Dressing

(Skip this section if you don't have any basement windows.)

When you think about waterproofing your basement and fixing it up, you should think about your basement windows.

There are three issues –

1. Do the windows leak water?.................................... *If so, we need to install drains.*
2. Are the windows rusted, rotted, drafty, or ugly? .... *If so, replace them.*
3. Are the window <u>wells</u> ugly, rusty, and open? .... *If so, replace them.*

If your basement windows leak when it rains hard, it's probably because of one of the following three reasons –

1. The gutters are overflowing into the window wells.
2. The ground around the window is pitched towards the house.
3. A downspout is dumping lots of water near the window.

They Aren't Submarine Windows

When there is water outside of a basement window, it will leak into the basement – afterall, they aren't submarine windows! So we need to fix them.

Besides the obvious – fix the gutters, regrade if possible, and extend the downspouts, if you don't do something else the window will likely leak again in the future. So the best thing to do is install a drain from the window well to the perimeter drainage system around your basement that leads to the sump pump.

A simple system called a WellDuct, a vertical extension of the WaterGuard System, drains water from the window well before the window leaks in the event that water rises in the well.

A drain hole is drilled through your basement wall just under the windowsill. If the wall is a block wall, the hole is lined with a section of pipe. Then a grate is installed on the outside over the hole. The WellDuct conduit itself is installed on the inside of your basement wall.

If water rises to threaten the window, it goes through the grate, through the wall, down the WellDuct, through your inside drain system, and to the sump pump. Simple.

It's a good idea to cover the grate with clean stone outside to keep leaves from plugging it – unless you have a SunHouse (keep reading).

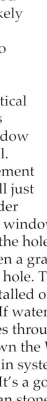

Everlasting Windows

If your windows look bad or are rotted or drafty – replace them.

Now is the time to do this. New "EverLast" energy-efficient, all-vinyl windows can be installed to replace your old ones. The new windows look much better, don't let wind in, have double-pane glass, and never need paint – perfect for the damp environment close to the ground.

A Perfect Basement Window.
Energy efficient and rot and mildew-resistant windows.

9

Important for

Finished Basements

What Are You Looking At?

If your window wells are rusty, ugly, or open at the top, they can be dramatically improved. Window wells without covers let in leaves and debris, and rain and gutter overflow water gets in. The dirt bottom allows weeds to grow and mud to splash up onto your windows. All this makes for a pretty lousy view from inside the basement – the space you want to improve.

9

You'll Love This!

The Answer is a Great Product Called SunHouse Basement Window Enclosures

The light-colored SunHouse window well, features a sturdy, clear cover that fits nicely and a bottom that prevents weed growth as well as keeps leaves, debris, and rain out. One of the SunHouse's best benefits is that with the clean, light-colored bottom a lot more sunlight bounces into your basement and brightens up a space where we can use *all the light we can get.*

WOW. *Look at all the light that SunHouse reflects onto the ceiling.*

You Choose.

Looks Great!
*The SunHouse Basement Window Enclosure really dresses up what used to be an eye-sore.
Bright and clean.*

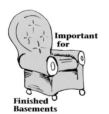

Important for
Finished Basements

"Carpenter Ready"

If you plan to finish your basement at anytime in the future, now is the time to address the basement windows and make your basement "Carpenter ready." Carpenters don't know a lot about *basement* windows, and nothing about window wells or the drainage of them. Not their bag baby! Have a waterproofing contractor who deals with these products everyday take care of it for you.

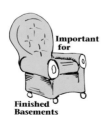

Important for
Finished Basements

Basement Bedroom Code

If you are making bedrooms in your basement, you need to check the local codes about "egress" window requirements. Basically, in case of a fire you need two ways out of a bedroom. The door is one, and a window big enough to climb out of and to the surface can be another.

Keep Windows Closed!

Even though EverLast basement windows are smooth-operating windows and easy to open, I can think of no reason to ever open a window in a basement other than to pass a long object, such as a ladder, through. In cooler weather we want to keep cold air out. In warm weather we want to keep warm air out to avoid condensation problems.

Chapter 10

Foundation Fractures
Fixing Wall Cracks

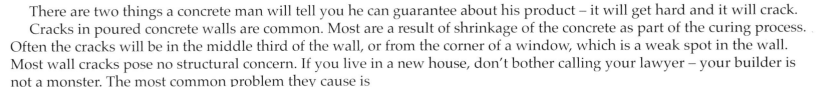

*(Skip this section if you have block walls, stone walls,
or if you have a poured foundation wall and don't have leaking wall cracks.)*

Concrete Cracks

There are two things a concrete man will tell you he can guarantee about his product – it will get hard and it will crack.

Cracks in poured concrete walls are common. Most are a result of shrinkage of the concrete as part of the curing process. Often the cracks will be in the middle third of the wall, or from the corner of a window, which is a weak spot in the wall. Most wall cracks pose no structural concern. If you live in a new house, don't bother calling your lawyer – your builder is not a monster. The most common problem they cause is water leaking through them.

You can fix them by digging it up and patching it outside. But that's a big hole, and it's messy. Whatever you patch it with can fail and if it re-leaks, what are you going to do – dig it up all over again? Also, there may be something in the way outside that prevents you from digging a big hole there – such as a driveway, sidewalk, deck, or porch.

Many methods have been developed over the years to fix wall cracks from the inside. Whenever you hear that "many methods have been developed over the years" to do anything, you have to conclude that people were not satisfied with the previous methods. This is true for crack repair.

The first thing to not do is try to patch a crack on the surface of the wall inside. Even if you chisel out the crack a bit before you jam in any miracle compound, your chances of success are slim. Why? Because wall cracks move. Changes in the soil, such as wet (swell) and dry (shrink), and hot and cold seasonal changes make the wall move, and the earth outside uses the crack as an expansion and contraction joint. So the miracle goo either cracks in the middle or loses its bond with the concrete and then re-leaks.

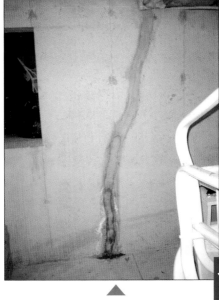

10

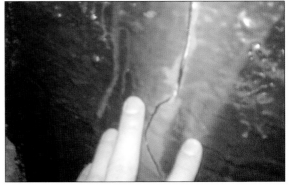

Recracked. *Rigid materials recrack with wall movement.*

A Common Sight. *A crack that has been repaired many times is still leaking.*

Another older, fairly popular method that's still used in some areas is to inject epoxy into the crack. Think of it as crazy glue – usually clear, goes in as a liquid, sticks good, and dries rock hard. The problem is that epoxy allows no flexibility for movement. When the wall wants to move, the epoxy can't, so it either breaks loose or a new crack develops.

To improve on this, someone invented a urethane liquid that could be injected into the crack and dry like a rubbery material. The logic is that this material was flexible so it would move with wall movement. Sounds good in theory. The problem is that a crack that is only $1/16$" can easily open to $1/8$" – which is 100% bigger. Unfortunately, urethane won't stretch that far. Not even close.

Another problem with injecting stuff into a crack is if there is dirt in a crack that washed in with the water, it prevents the stuff you inject from getting a good bond to the sides of the crack.

Non-Stick. *Dirt inside of a crack prevents injected sealant from sticking good.*

69

et me be realistic. All of the above methods for fixing a wall crack can work. But their track record shows they don't work ALL the time. And the more years that go by following the repair, the higher the percentage becomes that these repairs will re-leak.

Going on our premise that we only want to do things once, and that we want our basement dry all the time, we need to find a better way. It just so happens I know one. In fact, like a lot of the things you read in this book, I developed and patented it.

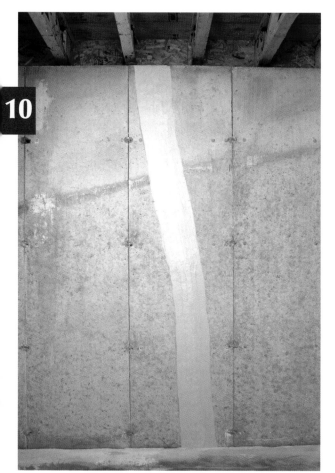

"FlexiSpan" Crack Repair Works Everytime

FlexiSpan seals the crack and provides a built-in secondary repair strategy in case the seal fails. First a small drywell is developed into the floor under the crack. If we can connect into the perimeter drainage system or a stone bed under the floor, great. If not, we make our own drywell about 5-10 gallons in size. Then we seal the crack with a urethane-based sealant (not the same urethane that we talked about being injected on the previous page). Next a special polyurethane ether foam strip is applied over the first seal. This foam strip is set up so water from within and behind it can drain into the drywell. Then it is overlaid with polyurethane sealant and tooled off to look like a gray colored drywall compound joint. Lastly, the opening in the floor is re-concreted.

Now your wall crack is sealed, and if any water ever gets past the seal, it drains down into the drywell. The results you are looking for – a dry wall and dry floor are achieved – forever – because FlexiSpan is…well, flexible. Very flexible, and no amount of wall movement will make it re-leak.

Flexible. *FlexiSpan gets results – a dry wall and a dry floor.*

FlexiSpan is a great innovation that works like a charm. It's especially appreciated in the Midwest where the wall movement can be even more substantial.

In some cases a crack may be injected with something and a FlexiSpan repair will be installed over it anyway to ensure there will be no problems in the future – ever! This may be done on a really bad leaker, or a very large crack.

Lots of Cracks? Opt for Full Protection

If you have lots of wall cracks, you may just consider installing a WaterGuard system and BrightWall paneling over your leaking wall cracks without doing anything else to them. This way if you discover floor/wall joint leakage in the future, you aren't starting from scratch to fix that problem. You can get a dry floor and dry walls in this manner. If you spent money to fix five wall cracks for example, you only have a warranty on those five wall cracks, not on the floor or any other wall imperfections.

A Better Solution. *With multiple wall cracks, install BrightWall paneling to drain leaks into a perimeter WaterGuard system.*

When Cracks are More than Cracks

If your cracks are very large, or if you run your finger across a foundation crack and it's uneven (one side higher than the other), you may want to get advice from a foundation structural repair contractor. Big cracks indicate wall buckling or vertical movement in your foundation, usually caused from clay soils swelling and shrinking. Your waterproofing contractor may be a structural repair contractor as well.

Leaking Pipe Penetrations

Leaking pipe penetrations can be dealt with in the same way as wall cracks. Pipes can have lots of movement in and out of the wall as they expand and contract along their length. All the same older methods have been done with pipes as with wall cracks. FlexiSpan can be done on a pipe penetration for a reliable, effective cure.

10

Chapter 11

Drinking Water Destruction
Common Plumbing Leaks

(Skip this section if you don't have a water heater or a washing machine.)

Important for
Finished Basements

Whether the water in your basement is from a groundwater leak or from a plumbing leak, the results are the same; with the exception that your homeowner's insurance company will pay for the damage from the plumbing leak. In fact, the number one type of claim that insurance companies pay out on homeowner's policies is water damage. And the top two types of water damage claims are from water heaters leaking and washing machine hoses bursting.

Water heaters don't last very long. During the life of a home the water heater will be replaced many times – and a common way that a water heater lets you know that it needs to be replaced is by leaking. When a water heater leaks it doesn't just empty out, it continues to leak because it continues to automatically refill itself. So it could leak for weeks if you don't notice. I have seen basements with many inches of water from water heater leaks.

Washing machine hoses are the other one. Do you shut that valve off behind your washing machine after every load? If you do, you're in the minority. Nobody ever does. So that means there is water pressure on the hoses to the washing machine all the time. You are using these cheap, $5 per pair, rubber hoses as permanent plumbing. And like a tired old garden hose laying in your garden, one day it's going to pfffffttttttttttt! Or worse it will gusshhhhhhhh when the end blows off and it swings around like a crazed snake! You can get 500 gallons an hour out of a washing machine hose at 50 psi pressure. I have seen water coming OUT of a basement window from a blown washing machine hose. Now that will ruin your tea party!

While you can't provide for a leak anywhere in your plumbing system, if there are some simple, low-cost things you can do to avoid the damage from these two most common eventualities, you should do it.

A Scene Repeated Every Day and Night in Homes Everywhere. *The start of a major flood from a water heater leaking.*

Here's What to Do

For water heater leaks – a product called FloodRing can be easily installed around your water heater. This 4-inch-high ring gets sealed to the floor, contains water heater leakage, and drains it to the perimeter drainage system that your waterproofing contractor will install. It doesn't cost much, and will one day pay for itself many times over.

Preventive Medicine. *FloodRing installed around a water heater protects against future leakage.*

For your washing machine hoses – Replace them with "FloodChek" hoses. These hoses are industrial-duty, triple-ply, 20-year warranted hoses with beefy machined brass end connections.

These two products are what I call the Domestic Water Flood Protection Program. It doesn't cost much, and makes a lot of sense.

Over Achiever. *FloodChek hoses believe they are hard plumbing.*

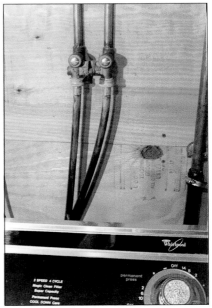

Can't Perform Under Pressure. *Cheap hoses don't withstand the pressure put on them for long.*

Chapter 12
Crawl Space Hell

(Skip this section if you don't have a crawl space.)

This subject is so important that I wrote a whole book about it called "Dirt Crawl Spaces – America's Housing Epidemic." If you have a crawl space, you should get this book from your local Basement Systems dealer or CleanSpace installer.

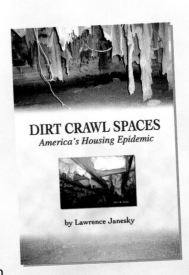

DIRT CRAWL SPACES
America's Housing Epidemic

by Lawrence Janesky

There is only one cause of all the problems in crawl spaces – Relative Humidity. When it's high it causes:

✔ Mold to grow
✔ Your floor to rot
✔ Makes a haven for insects of all sorts
✔ Causes odors
✔ Wastes energy by increasing heating and cooling costs
✔ Can cause all the above effects upstairs and throughout the house
✔ And these things affect your property value – who wants to buy a house with a problem?

High Relative Humidity causes all these bad things, and there are a few things that cause high Relative Humidity.

✔ Leaking groundwater through your crawl space walls that lays there and soaks the soil.
✔ Exposed earth on the floor of the crawl space.
✔ Open vents to the outside.

So What Do We Do?

For the groundwater we install a sump pump system (same considerations as Chapter 5) and make sure the water leaking in gets to it instead of ponding.

For the wet walls and exposed earth we install the patented CleanSpace crawl space encapsulation system.

For the open vents – we close them – permanently with CleanSpace Vent Covers.

Look Ma, No Mold. *CleanSpace is formulated with the* Ultra-Fresh *anti-microbial agent to resist mold and bacteria growth.*

You'll Love This!

The CleanSpace crawl space encapsulation system is a heavy duty 7-layer liner material; like a pool liner. It gets installed across the floor and up the walls and sealed around all piers and pipes, etc. It stops all the water vapor from the walls or soil and is very durable – so you can't poke holes in it, rip it, or pull it down off the walls when you crawl in there – and yes, you'll have no problem crawling into your crawl space once the CleanSpace liner is installed, it's that clean, bright white, and nice! It will also last as long as the house. Besides that, it looks fantastic! Talk about a crawl space makeover!

Heaven and Hell. *A CleanSpace system turns crawl space Hell into crawl space Heaven.*

What About the Vents?

Important

Vents are sealed with vent covers installed outside. The building code required these vents when your home was built. The building code was wrong and made your problem worse by letting in hot, humid air in the summer, which causes condensation and rot and mold. In the winter these vents let in freezing cold air, making your floors upstairs cold and wasting energy. The building codes are now changing, and in the future vented dirt crawl spaces will be a thing of the past.

Again for more info, get my book on Dirt Crawl Spaces. This is the Reader Digest version.

Seal All Air Leaks to the Outside

When a CleanSpace system is installed, you want to seal vents to keep out evil unconditioned outside air. But vents aren't the only way outside air can get into your crawl space. Spaces under the sill plate and around pipes and wires to the outside, poorly fitting or rotted hatch doors, and other odd openings are all paths that need to be sealed to get the best results.

One area that was previously ignored is the open cavities in the top of block walls. Block walls are most common in dirt crawl spaces. Outside air goes right through porous block walls and up out of the top of the wall into the inside of the crawl space. To seal the top of the block walls, a product called "CleanSpace Wall Cap" works great. It's an "L"-shaped molding that slips right on top of the block wall covering the space the sill plate does not. The clear plastic allows for termite inspections without removing it.

Provide for Plumbing Leaks in Your Crawl Space

Important

In a dirt crawl space a plumbing leak will leak into the dirt forever (because you'll never notice it), keeping the dirt wet and the humidity up. When a CleanSpace system is installed, a plumbing leak can fill up your crawl space like a swimming pool. The sump systems described in Chapter 5, SuperSump and TripleSafe, have airtight lids with airtight floor drains that drain water from the top of the CleanSpace liner in the event of a plumbing leak in your crawl space.

If you don't have groundwater leakage you won't need a sump system in your crawl space with your CleanSpace system. However, you still need to provide for plumbing leaks. You can do this with a SmartDrain.

A SmartDrain is a drywell-type unit that gets installed in your crawl space along with the CleanSpace liner. It features an alarm and an airtight floor drain in its lid. In the event of a plumbing leak, the alarm sounds alerting you to the leak, and the water drains away into the soil under the CleanSpace until you get the leak fixed.

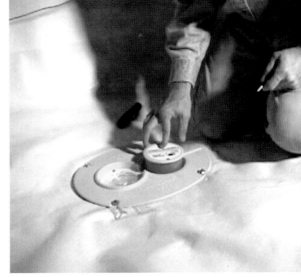

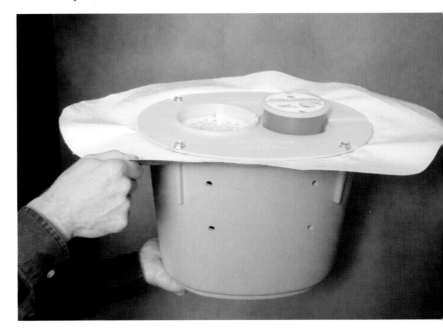

Your Crawl Space Access Door Should Seal Tight

Many crawl spaces have an access door to the outside. Most often it is made of plywood, and because it's down by the ground it rots easily. These rotted warped doors usually seal poorly and look like heck. The answer is an all-plastic door – that won't rot, warp, or need paint, and bugs won't eat it. Perfect.

Knobs screw into anchors in the wall to draw the door tight against weather-stripping to seal off outside air.

Before. *A rotting, loose-fitting, warped plywood door lets in lots of air.*

After. *A snug-fitting, all-plastic door stops air and moisture from entering.*

You'll Love This!

Fixing Your Crawl Space Pays for Itself

A vented dirt crawl space is a huge energy waster. The outside air constantly flowing into your home increases the heat and air conditioning load. And the dampness needs to be wrung out of the air by your air conditioning system, which puts a heavy tax on it – and you. It costs you real dollars in energy bills, not to mention the cost of wood replacement, mold clean-up, and property-value reduction.

An independent study revealed that homeowners who properly fix their vented dirt crawl space can save 10% to 20% on their heating and air conditioning costs! In my opinion, if the conditions are right (meaning all wrong before the installation), you can save more than that. CleanSpace is one of those things that you are going to pay for whether you get it or not. That makes it a no-brainer to get it.

Crawl Space Insulation

If you are going to insulate or re-insulate your crawl space, it's better to insulate the walls with two-inch foam insulation than to stuff fiberglass between the floor joists. The foam insulation can be put on under or over the CleanSpace liner.

Dehumidifying Your Crawl Space

Once a sump system and a CleanSpace liner are installed, and the vents are closed, the "cherry on top" is a dehumidification system. In Chapter 8 we described a lot about this issue and using a super-duper unit called a SaniDry Basement Air System. This system comes in a lower height unit for crawl spaces called SaniDry CSB.

Remember it's not just the crawl space (or basement) you are dehumidifying. Because air rises from the bottom to top of your home, the air that now rises will dry your house instead of wetting it.

Another way to dry the air in your crawl space is to "condition" it. This means you use the Heating and Air Conditioning System to heat, cool, and dry the crawl space. Because your crawl space is low it doesn't really tax your system very much at all. In fact, because warm air rises to heat the floors above, it costs almost nothing as long as you have a complete CleanSpace system installed and seal the vents and other air openings to the outside.

One way to condition a crawl space is to constantly blow a small amount of air from upstairs into the crawl space. You can do this with a "Crawl-O-Sphere air machine." Depending on the size of your crawl space, this system draws from between 15 and 80 cubic feet of air per minute from the upstairs and blows it into your crawl space. The air from upstairs is dry in the summer (if you have central air conditioning) and warm and dry in the winter, and for little cost, will dry your crawl space pretty well. It is not as effective as a SaniDry, but the Crawl-O-Sphere machine is a lower-cost alternative.

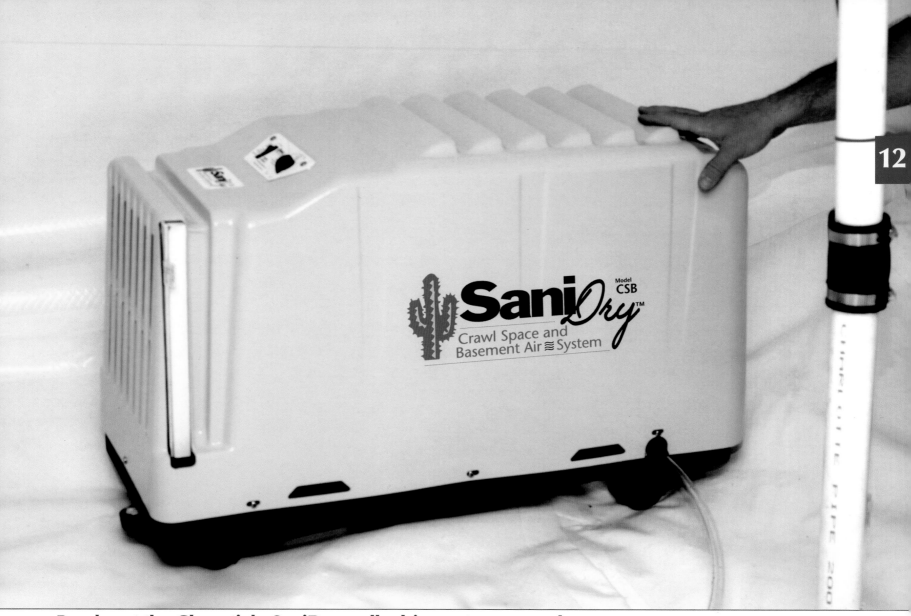

Break out the Chapstick. SaniDry really dries out your crawl space.
SaniDry CSB's low profile, air filtration, and heavy-duty drying make this the perfect
crawl space dehumidifier.

Chapter 13

Promises, Promises
Warranties and Service

B y now, you probably realize the myriad options available to you in basement waterproofing, and those options offer various levels of protection against water leaking into your basement. While hiring a contractor, who is an authorized Basement Systems dealer, will get you what you pay for, one thing is for sure, no matter who you hire, you will never get what you ***don't*** pay for.

There are two sides to a transaction. Besides what the seller sells, there is what the buyer buys. Many times the buyer wants to get away with spending less with overly optimistic hopes of achieving a dry space and then being able to use it. It can work for a time, but one day, in nearly all cases, the buyer discovers that he was wrong in being frugal – to a fault.

Truth in Waterproofing

The reality is – there are no guarantees. A guarantee is saying something won't happen. A professional basement waterproofing contractor can not say your basement will never flood again. What he or she can warrant is that if your basement does leak, and it was because of this happening or that happening, then this is what he or she will do for you.

Of course, the warranty depends on what you buy. If water leaks in from an area of your basement that was not specifically addressed, then it is not covered and you will get a proposal for the additional work and expense required to address it.

It is important to understand that a warranty from your basement waterproofing contractor is not a guarantee and not insurance. For example, if you buy a new car, and the car breaks down, you won't be compensated for the fact that you missed your sister's wedding or a day of work because of it. If your basement floods and your stuff

gets wet and ruined, it is not covered by your warranty. What is covered is that if additional work is required to get a result that you should have achieved from the work you bought, then it will be provided at no charge.

The waterproofing contractor has no control over what you put in the basement. Some people don't put much in their basements. Others install a beautiful finished basement with a home theater system. The stakes are high. This is why all the issues discussed in this book are so very important. There is never any complete guarantee you won't get flooded again. There are so many variables in a home's construction – soils, water problems, and what people do – that you simply can't say for certain that you will never get flooded again.

However, by choosing the right contractor to do the right things, you can reduce the chance of ever getting flooded again to a statistically insignificant number, and have a great shot at never facing water damage in your below-grade space again. Little reason exists as to why you can't have a basement reliably dry enough from which to make comfortable finished space.

13

Bluntly Speaking

❖ Damage to your belongings is not covered.
❖ Damage to your carpeting or walls is not covered.
❖ Most homeowners insurance does not cover groundwater leaks and the damage from a groundwater leak.
❖ Mold growing is not covered by your warranty.
❖ If you only have part of your basement treated, your warranty is very limited.
❖ A proper waterproofing system with a SaniDry Basement Air System will stop mold, but it's not a warranty.
❖ If you have a single pump system, you will get flooded one day.
❖ If you have a TripleSafe pump system your chances of getting flooded are tiny, but not zero.
❖ The floor and walls are two different things with two different warranties.
> ❖ There will be some dust from the installation – sometimes not much at all, sometimes a lot, maybe it will get upstairs, but often just some in the basement itself.
> ❖ The discharge location can be changed at extra cost later if you find you are not happy with where the water is going. This is not a big deal and usually doesn't cost a lot.

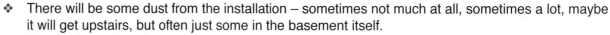

Help Yourself

❖ Don't skimp – do it right even though it costs more.
❖ Hire a Basement Systems dealer, since you won't find the solutions in this book anywhere else.
❖ Report any problems to your contractor right away.
❖ Annual service is recommended. It doesn't cost much to find a problem before it finds you. When your dealer contacts you to tell you it's time for annual maintenance – schedule it.

Chapter 14

The Perfect Basement
If Money's No Object, Then Do This

Money is an object!

Okay, it is. But only if you expected to pay cash for this repair. Most people don't pay cash for an automobile – they finance it. There are all kinds of options to get your basement fixed right – a home equity loan, credit cards, or a home improvement loan with which your dealer can help you.

If a house is worth owning for what you paid for it, with a wet unusable lower level that causes property damage, frustration, anger and despair, then it is worth owning with a dry usable space for what you paid for it plus $15,000. Make sense?

You'll Love This!

The Perfect System. *A WaterGuard perimeter drainage system with a TripleSafe sump pump system, BrightWall paneling, and a SaniDry basement air system. Ahhhh!*

Patent Notices-

Many of the products and systems discussed in this book are patented or patent pending by Basement Systems Inc.

Basement Environment Specialists®

1-800-640-1500

These include but are not limited to –

WaterGuard System

SuperSump System

TripleSafe System

IceGuard System

WaterWatch Alarm System

Sealed Sump Lid with air-tight floor drain

CleanPump Stand

RainChute

ThermalDry Floor Matting

FlexiSpan Crack Repair

WellDuct Drain System

FloodRing

CleanSpace

CleanSpace Vent Covers

SmartDrain

CleanSpace Wall Cap

Crawl Space Replacement Door

Crawl-O-Sphere Air System

About the Author

After five years as a carpenter and builder, Larry Janesky founded Basement Systems Inc. in 1987 to provide basement waterproofing services to existing homes. He soon learned that there was much room for improvement in the industry, and set out to make those improvements. He has since patented 21 products, with more pending and even more in various stages of design and development.

Larry is currently the president of the world's largest basement waterproofing and crawl space repair dealer network, Basement Systems Inc., that specializes in developing and providing products that result in dry below-ground environments. The company has won three business ethics awards, two consumer education awards, and multiple quality and innovation awards in the past five years.

Larry has been invited to a number of industry conventions to discuss his research and solutions. Larry has trained more than 3000 people over the last 16 years on basement waterproofing and crawl space repair. His articles have been published in *Fine Homebuilding* magazine, *Permanent Buildings and Foundations* magazine, and other publications. He wrote the book on dirt crawl spaces entitled, "Dirt Crawl Spaces: America's Housing Epidemic."

Larry enjoys his free time in rural Connecticut with his son Tanner, daughters Chloe and Autumn, and his lovely wife Wendy. There he also builds and rides on his motocross track and ATV trails.

You can read more about Basement Systems Inc., basement waterproofing, below-grade environments, and the CleanSpace® Crawl Space Encapsulation™ System, at www.basementsystems.com.

Notes

Notes